TREASURE IN EARTHEN VESSELS
The Church as a Human Community

James M. Gustafson

TREASURE IN EARTHEN VESSELS

The Church as a Human Community

The University of Chicago Press
Chicago and London

The University of Chicago Press, Chicago 60637
The University of Chicago Press, Ltd., London

Published 1961 by Harper & Brothers. Midway Reprint 1976
Printed in the United States of America

International Standard Book Number: 0-226-31106-6

To my parents

John Otto Gustafson
Edith Moody Gustafson

Contents

Preface

Several purposes and interests have governed the writing of this book. It is a study of the Church, mainly in the light of social thought. But it always has in view the relation of social interpretation to theological interpretation of the Church.

The guiding purposes in this effort can be stated simply. I have tried to understand as much of life in the Church as possible, and particularly its "unity" and "continuity" (more precisely, its social and historical consistency) within a nondoctrinal framework. The "natural" processes that the Church has in common with other human communities provide the principles of interpretation in the bulk of the analysis. Jesus Christ, the Bible, Holy Communion, etc. are interpreted in terms of their social function in the Church.

This has been done for several reasons. Basic is the personal one that lies at the heart of what every writer does—the problems and possibilities of this approach are issues that are important to me, and are a part of my way of working in ethics, sociology of religion, and theology. But more important, the essay seeks to show by implication how confinement of the discussion to traditional doctrinal terms inherently oversimplifies and distorts the Church—that which the theologian seeks to understand. This essay shows the extent to which principles from the social sciences and social philosophy can account for that which also can be accounted for in doctrinal language. For example, unity and continuity are interpreted in terms of social processes, and not in terms of the presence of Christ, or the work of the Holy Spirit. Thus it is an argument against theological oversimplification, and for the importance of using nondoctrinal points of view in theological discussion. The root convictions about theological method that lie behind this emphasis are not here developed.

But as a member of the Christian community I find that the exclusive use of principles from social science and philosophy does not satisfactorily interpret life in the Church. The social processes do not fully explain the meaning of Christian life in the Church. Thus a sociological oversimplification is as inadequate as a theological one. This poses the problem dealt with briefly in Chapter 8, namely, the relation between theological and social interpretation, or, how that which can be understood in terms of nature and history can be a means or agency of what is more than natural and historical in its meaning and its source.

Thus the book expresses a conversation in which I believe most Christians in the modern world are involved, namely, between ourselves as participants in a world of naturalistic and scientific explanations, and ourselves as believers in God revealed in Jesus Christ.

There are many subordinate purposes in various chapters. Some of them can be subsumed under one aim, namely, to show that the historical and social relativity of the Church is part of its essential character. This is so in a double sense. This relativity is of the essence of its nature as an historical community, and it is essential to the achievement of its purpose in the world. The Church *is* an "earthen vessel," and its character as earthen vessel *makes it effective.* (The title of the book was suggested by a memorable sermon preached by my colleague, Julian N. Hartt, in which he explored the nature and function of earthen vessels, i.e., pots and pans, in portraying the nature and purpose of the Church.) The Church is *earthen*—of the stuff of natural and historical life. The Church is a *vessel*, it is useful. The contact with man and culture is made through the social and historical media of the Church—its natural functions, political forms, etc.

The Appendix is included to show in a more technical way how the framework which guides the central section of the book was developed in the context of philosophical issues that are involved.

My indebtedness to others is great. The manuscript was completed during the first part of a leave from normal academic duties made possible by the generosity of the Guggenheim Foundation and Yale University. To those institutions, and to the University of Lund, Sweden, which provided the setting for my work, I am grateful. The Appendix, and the point of view that gives the argument its character, are taken in part from my dissertation for the Ph.D. degree at Yale University. Therefore, those institutions that aided my graduate study deserve thanks.

The men of past and present generations by whose books and articles I have been provóked to reflect about the Church are formally acknowledged in footnotes. To living teachers who have interested me in these authors, and who in our conversations through a decade and more have encouraged me to pursue the combination of interests expressed in this book, I happily acknowledge an obligation. James Luther Adams stimulated my interest in Ernst Troeltsch, Max Weber, Wilhelm Dilthey, and Karl Mannheim, and thus introduced me to a tradition of social interpretation deeply imbedded in my work. Kenneth Underwood encouraged my studies of churches as social organizations, and his main assistance is reflected in Chapter 3. Since I first read

The Meaning of Revelation and *Social Sources of Denominationalism*, H. Richard Niebuhr has been my mentor in many ways. He helped me set in theological context my interests in social science and social philosophy gained as an undergraduate. He led me to a serious study of Henri Bergson and Josiah Royce; he revived my interest in George Herbert Mead and Charles Horton Cooley; and he encouraged my studies in the sociology of knowledge in relation to the Church, ethics, and theology. Parts of this book are hardly more than an elaboration of ideas he has expressed.

Others have criticized the contents of this essay in various of its previous spoken and written forms. To my colleagues, to my students, and to my friends from graduate school days, I am grateful. Docent Berndt Gustafsson of Lund read the entire manuscript and made helpful suggestions. Louise, who believes she has not helped, has been a willing, understanding, and encouraging companion and aid through all the studies, writing, editing, and proofreading that take this present, awesomely irrevocable form.

James Gustafson

TREASURE IN EARTHEN VESSELS
The Church as a Human Community

CHAPTER I

The Church:
a Human Community

The Task: a social interpretation of the Church

Athough there has been much writing and discussion about the nature of the Church in recent years, one approach has been neglected. There has been little interpretation of the Church in the light of social theory. Books and articles abound about the Church which use the concepts and language of Christian doctrine and Biblical exegesis. Expositions of the Biblical view of the Church have been made by New Testament scholars and systematic theologians. The issue of the relation of Jesus Christ to the Church has occupied the attention of many of the best minds in Christendom. Under the auspices of the World Council of Churches, Baptism, Holy Communion, ordination, liturgy and other specific aspects of Church life have been subjected to many inquiries. In the theological conversation about the nature of the Church there are many passing references to the fact that the Church is a human community and institution, but the main attention has been given to a doctrinal understanding of the "essence" of the Church, or to the relation of the Church to the persons of the Trinity. Efforts to take the social nature of the Christian community seriously in theological discourse are rare. The present essay seeks to contribute to the theological discussions by focusing on the Church as an historical, human community.[1]

While the theological treatises have tended to ignore social theory, the sociological studies of the Church have often been confined to very specific problems. They have not emphasized theory. The literature in which the Christian community is subjected to rigorous sociological analysis is growing. Studies of cities and towns contribute to an

---

[1] The word "community" at this point and throughout most of the book is used in a very loose sense. It refers to a body of persons who share some measure of common life, and a common loyalty. At a later point the word "fellowship" is introduced in contrast to "institution."

The word "church" is capitalized where it refers to the whole Christian community. Where it refers to particular denominations, congregations, or movements, it is in lower case type.

understanding of the interaction between religious behavior and social stratification, cultural values, and population movements. Studies of the ministry clarify the problems of the role of the clergyman in Church and secular society. Studies have been made of organizational aspects of denominations that are comparable to studies of government agencies and corporations. With the focus of attention necessarily defined by very specific data, such research has tended to ignore the development of a social theory of the Church.

In addition to sociological examinations of particular aspects of Church life, there are distinguished historical studies that are sociologically informed. The works of Ernst Troeltsch and Max Weber, for example, bring the history of Christianity under the light of sociological motifs and concepts. Social and cultural predispositions which make a particular society receptive to certain forms of Christianity, and in turn color its expressions of religious life, have been delineated. The causal efficacy of religious beliefs within the complex patterns of modern historical development has been noted, as in Weber's famous thesis about the inner affinity of the Protestant ethic and the spirit of capitalism. In view of the grand sweep of historical data that men like Troeltsch and Weber had in mind, the more reflective elements that constitute a theory of Christian community sometimes come to the fore. The distinction between the church type, sect type, and mystical type of religious society is an example. But the primary intention of these works has not been to develop an interpretation of the Church as a human community; rather it has been to illuminate its history.

A social interpretation of the Church is necessarily hard to place within the traditional division of academic disciplines. If the task of developing it were assigned to a systematic theologian, the result might be a deductive scheme of concepts, resting finally on basic dogmas of the Church, and merely pointing toward the historical community. Should a secular sociologist undertake the work he might lack the information, sensitivity, and empathy required to create an adequate theory of the Church as it is known by Christian believers. A philosopher can point to the constitutive elements in any theoretical framework, and his reflections on history, or on the state, might shed light on the Church. But he is not likely to begin with the experience of Christianity as the object of his thought. An historian is more likely to attend to the gathering of accurate information and the illuminating interpretation of it. His discipline restrains him from engaging in the risks of generalization. The professional workers from each discipline are likely to look askance at the whole effort, for a social interpretation of the Church intrudes into areas where specialization has rightful claims.

The enterprise thus is fraught with difficulties. Nevertheless it is important. The Church can be defined as a human community with an historical continuity identifiable by certain beliefs, ways of work, rites, loyalties, outlooks, and feelings. Whatever else the Church is to the systematic theologian and Biblical exegete, it is a people with a history. It is a social entity with temporal and spatial dimensions. It is human, and shares many characteristics of other human communities such as nations, trade unions, and professions. As a human community it is subject to various modes of study and interpretation.

One student may be concerned with the ultimate meaning, purpose, and status of this community in the divine plan. He will ask about its relation to the work of the Holy Spirit; to the person and work of Jesus Christ; to the ultimate fulfillment of history in the coming of the Kingdom of God. The framework of interpretation is largely couched in the traditional language of Christian doctrine. His answers will have some implications for a social interpretation but cannot provide its basic viewpoint.

Another may look at the human community of Christians and its history in order to find its changing patterns of life and thought. He will ask what historical alterations have taken place in its liturgy and polity, in its doctrine and understanding of mission; or what factors from within and outside the community seem to be important in conditioning the changes that have taken place. The information required for such investigations is specific; documents of many sorts are the data. The task of the historian involves the interpretation of the history of the community. Any social interpretation of the Church must be somewhat informed by what Church historians have written. But the task of developing such an interpretation is not identical with the historian's task.

A third student may properly determine narrow temporal and spatial limits within which he will investigate the Church. He may choose to study the congregations in a particular city over a decade of rapid social change. He may ask who attends what churches; what correlations exist between religious beliefs, social status, and political affiliation; and what religious life appears to do for the people of a given town. The information to be analyzed is very detailed; the procedures of investigation must be tested by the canons of good scholarship in the social sciences. A social interpretation must be informed by studies made by sociologists and anthropologists, but its author must speculate and generalize beyond what is verified by detailed local studies.

The historical Christian community has developed patterns of authority and processes of decision-making. It has taken an organizational shape comparable to other institutions. This invites the curiosity of another kind of student. He asks how social power is gained and exercised in the churches; what patterns of government prevail, and how they are related to the beliefs about God on the one hand and the necessity to work in a particular society on the other. Concepts from political science and the sociological studies of bureaucracy illumine the patterns of life in the Christian community. To ignore the organizational structure of this community is to miss an important part of its social character. Yet the social interpreter must be more inclusive, for the community is more than its political order.

Philosophers have also contributed to the understanding of human communities, particularly some who are rooted in nineteenth-century idealism. The temporal or historical continuity of human communities evokes questions about their nature. History seems to be a social and psychological experience. The nature of time is bound up with the experience of society and history. The subjective, inner unity of human communities evokes speculation about the essence of human togetherness. Atomistic views of man with their concomitant views of society based on mechanistic analogies seem inadequate. Other analogies are needed, more organic in character. Man has to be understood in his inner relatedness to other men, and not merely in external relations. A community has a *Volksgeist*, its life expresses a *Zeitgeist*; it has spiritual dimensions. Such reflections and speculations are often abstract. Yet, if critically used, they help to understand the nature of nations and religious communities, and the historical process in general. Philosophies of time and community reflect man's participation in, and experience of, human society. As such they can aid the social interpreter in understanding the nature of existence in the historical Christian community. But a social interpretation of the Church needs elements other than a philosophy of time and community.

The audacity of the social interpreter of the Church is obvious. He must be informed by concepts from several disciplines, yet it is possible that he does not qualify as a practitioner in any of them. But the risk is necessary. While a social analysis of the Church is not an exercise in Christian doctrine, it would be inadequate without some knowledge of doctrine, and of the other disciplines involved. It is not his goal to include every pertinent insight from all the disciplines; such completeness is impossible, and such eclecticism lacks unity of perspective and focus of interpretation. The point of view cannot be simply validated by the particular canons of sociology or systematic theology, history, or philosophy. It must stand finally on its own feet, and find its validity in whatever light it sheds upon the Christian community. What can be understood from the standpoint of the social theory may not be as easily observed from the standpoints of other disciplines. A social analysis of the Church does not displace investigation from other points of view, or interpretation through other concepts. It seeks merely to make a contribution to our understanding of the community of Christians, with its continuity through history, and its identity across culture barriers and space.

The Bias: the Church is an historical community

The writer of a social analysis of the Church assumes that there is continuity between the Christian community and other human communities. Common-sense observation makes this indisputable: people gather in appropriate buildings; churches have social hierarchies and political arrangements for the conduct of their affairs; an identifiable historical continuity exists through many generations and centuries; Christians have a common object of loyalty that binds them together. In these respects and others, similarities exist between the Christian community and the state, the nation, voluntary associations for charitable purposes, and many other groups and movements. There may be an irreducible uniqueness, a differentium that distinguishes the Church from all other historical communities, but this does not make it absolutely different in kind. It is subject to the same social and historical processes as other communities, and thus to the same types of investigation. Many of the concepts that illumine the nature of secular communities also illumine the nature of the Church.

Does the assumption of continuity between the Church and other forms of human community make a social analysis of the Church irrelevant to theology? By focusing on the Church as an historical community does one necessarily reduce it to an entity different from what the theologians talk about? The answer to these questions depends upon what one takes as his data for theological reflection about the Church. If the primary or exclusive datum of Christian theology is the Bible, and the theologian's task is an exegesis and exposition of texts, the present essay is not a theological document. If, however, the task of theology with reference to the Church is to come to some understanding of a social reality known in human experience, this essay is theological, or at least has implications for theology. Without systematic defense of a theological method, one must declare his principles of approach. Operationally at this point, the Church is defined as *an historically continuous body of persons known as Christians,* whose common life is in part institutionalized in churches. The Church is a social entity, with temporal and spatial boundaries. The inquirer, whether he be known as a theologian or a social theorist, has the task of understanding the nature of this community. What principles of interpretation aid in understanding the phenomenon called the Christian community? Reflective participants seek to understand the nature of any community in which they live. If they seek exclusively the differentium of that community, they lack an adequate understanding of it. If they think exclusively in the community's own characteristic language, e.g., the Biblical concepts, they will not see many phases of their own existence. Concepts from sociology and philosophy enlighten aspects of the life of the Church that traditional doctrinal or Biblical concepts do not.

The need for social thinking about the Church can be seen in relation to some recent theological treatises on ecclesiology. One example is the writing of Professor T. F. Torrance. If one thinks of the Church as an historical community, "form" and "order" denote patterns of its life that are experienced and at least in part can be described sociologically. In the jargon of a contemporary theologian, however, the ideas of form and order seem to refer primarily to something outside the realm of history and society. Professor Torrance, in a discussion of the meaning of "the body of Christ," asserts that in the Eucharist Christ is present bodily, and that there the Church becomes the Body of Christ in the profoundest sense.

With the Body of Christ the form of that Body is given and maintained. Church order is this form of the Body, and orders belong therefore to the form of the Church given to it as it engages in the communion of the Body and Blood of Christ, as it carries out the ordinance of the Lord, the Head of the Body. Thus in the Eucharist the Church assumes true form and order in obedience to the Word, but as such that order is not static, but dynamic, not a state but action.[2]

[2] T. F. Torrance, *Royal Priesthood,* Edinburgh, 1955, p. 72. Much more literature could be cited, e.g., J. A. T. Robinson, *The Body,* London, 1952, and Anders

From the point of view of a social analyst a number of questions must be answered before such a statement begins to be meaningful. Is the Body of Christ identical with the historical community of Christians? If it is not identical, precisely what is the relationship? Do the form and order of the Body have any reference to historical structures in the life of the Christian community? Or is the reference to something more like form or idea in Plato's philosophy? If this is the case how does social order in the Church participate in its "true form" in the Body? From the point of view of a social interpretation the fundamental difficulties of a statement like Torrance's lie in its lack of clarity in the meaning of words and its abstractness. It is removed from what most Christians refer to when they think of the Church, i.e., a body of people, a social movement. The Church has political operations; how are we to understand these? The Church meets natural and social needs of man. The Church has historical continuity and inner social unity. How are these to be understood? If one answers only in terms meaningful to the properly initiated theologian, not much has been explained, and not much understood.[3]

The Direction: from the common toward the unique

Some aspects of the life of the Christian community have much in common with all human communities. The way in which it meets some of the natural needs of man—for example, providing an acceptable social fellowship—is continuous with the way in which other groups fulfill the same function. There are differentiating factors that distinguish the fellowship of the Church, at least normatively, from the fellowship of the residential neighborhood. In the beginning, however, it is important to see the continuities. Thus an examination of the

Nygren, *Christ and His Church*, Philadelphia, 1956, especially pp. 93-107. I have not maintained a continuing polemic against such theological interpretations throughout this book, though one is implied.

[3] Four contemporary theological essays are congenial to the spirit of the present one, though not identical with it. H. R. Niebuhr, in *The Purpose of the Church and Its Ministry*, New York, 1956, especially pp. 17-27, outlines a view of the Church that includes social dimensions within a theological perspective. Daniel T. Jenkins, in *Tradition and the Spirit*, London, 1951, and Albert Outler, in *The Christian Tradition and the Unity We Seek*, New York, 1957, both deal theologically with the continuity of the Church. These significant contributions are supplemented by the present essay through its use of nondoctrinal concepts to interpret the same process. Jenkins' concept of "traditioning" in part refers to a social psychological process. Claude Welch, in *The Reality of the Church*, New York, 1958, has a comprehensive view of the nature of the Church, and especially his Chap. II is congenial to the present work.

natural basis of community, including Christian community, is required. Whatever the intention of the Church may be in relating men to God, there are unintended consequences that are related to man's physical and social needs. Perhaps the specific intentions of the Christian community can be actualized only insofar as some of the natural needs of men are also fulfilled. A church fellowship meal in ancient or modern times illustrates this. Profound religious interpretations can be given to its significance: Jesus Christ is present in the breaking of bread together as he was at Emmaus, or the breaking of bread is a common remembrance of Jesus Christ, or it symbolizes the way in which the realm of the natural can be transformed and sanctified. But it is also based upon a very simple fact, namely, man's need for the continuation and nourishment of his bodily state.

Life in the Church meets some of the same natural needs that life in the family, or the economic order, or educational institutions also meet. The cultural anthropologists have interpreted the human functions of various phases of religious life in less complex societies such as those in the Trobriand Islands, Western Australia, and the American Southwest. Their theories can aid our understanding of how Christian Church life serves the common needs of men. Christians tend to resist such an interpretation; it seems to profane sacred things. Morally, however, it often unmasks Christian pretensions to uniqueness or profundity. (Such moral unmasking, however, is not the purpose of the present essay.) An adequate social interpretation of the Church must understand its natural basis.

Natural communities are always institutionalized. In order to continue in existence certain relationships and patterns of social order must be established. Each family, while lacking a written constitution and by-laws, nevertheless works out a pattern through which the decisions are made and actions taken that are required for its stability. The pattern may invest power in the father, or it may disperse it in a democratic way, but the pattern exists. In this sense some political processes take place within every family. The nation finds a more complex pattern necessary in order to keep its peace and engage in action commensurate with the common interest. The state becomes its political expression. The Christian community is not radically different from these or other natural communities. Decisions must be made about how the Church will execute its understanding of its purpose. Resources of men and money must be allocated. These actions necessarily involve political processes. The Church is a political community.

The intention of its political activity differs from that of the state; a different purpose exercises control over the ends to be achieved and the acceptable means for their achievement. The meaning of its activity may differ; in the Church men are presumably self-consciously seeking an order through which they can express their faith in God. But the political processes are essentially the same in both the gathering of men in loyalty to the nation and the gathering of men in loyalty to Jesus Christ. Christians have difficulty in accepting the reality of "Church politics," particularly in the United States where politics seems to have morally bad connotations. But social power is exercised, whether authorized or not, in every organized form of the Christian community. The local congregation, the denomination, and the World Council of Churches are all political institutions. Insight into the nature of the Church as a society comes from an understanding of the political processes common to all human communities. Particularly important is an understanding of the characteristic politics of the immediate environment of a particular church; for example, American churches are more lay-controlled than the churches of some other countries, in a manner comparable to democratic voluntary associations. Analysis of such features seems to many Christians to reduce the stature of the Church and its leaders, and thus defensiveness emerges. But the Church, as a human society, *is* a political community and can be analyzed as such for the purposes of a social study.

Communities are in part designated by the common language of their members, as philosophers and anthropologists have pointed out. A common language is often listed as one of the marks of a nation. A common technical language that can be used meaningfully in speech and writing marks to some extent the boundaries of a particular professional community. Those who know the language belong to the community; those who do not know it are outside. This is as true for the historical Christian community as it is for the German nation, or for the fellowship of physicians. The language that brings men together is not always one associated with a nation; it is often words and concepts that can be translated into many national languages. The basis of unity lies not so much in certain words as in meanings that are conveyed by different words to those who are properly initiated. A catechism, for example, gives a common language to the persons who receive instruction according to it. Confirmation based upon catechetical instruction is recognition that one understands certain concepts and meanings associated with the distinctive beliefs of the Christian community.

A Greek word, a German word, and an English word can represent the unity of the Christian community because a common meaning is conveyed by them. Sin, redemption, the cross, resurrection, justification, covenant: these are examples of the language of the Church.

Belonging to the Christian community means knowing its common language. The Church is a community because communication within it occurs through common verbal symbols. As a community of language the Church is like other communities. The differentiation lies in the key words and meanings that mark its life from that of other communities. The processes of internalizing meaning through the use of words are the same for Christian and other groups. The identity and continuity of the Church depend in part upon the process of communication, and the retention of key words through the course of history.

Verbal and other symbols, however, do not become personally meaningful to members of a community by a simple process of repetition and incantation. Symbols require interpretation. The national flag is more than colored cloth; it represents the unity of the nation. But its representative character is known only through the interpretation of its significance to each generation. Biblical language, the cross, and other objective signs require interpretation before their meaning becomes personal for the members of the Church. In the nation there are interpreters who take the charter and symbols of its life and relate their meaning to changing events and new generations. In the Christian community a comparable interpretive process also goes on. The signs or objective marks of the community must be interpreted to its members, and to those who move toward membership. The ethos of the surrounding community, e.g., its thought forms and art forms, is interpreted by the Church in the light of its special communal signs. The meaning of these signs remains relatively fixed, for meanings have a concrete reference point in creeds, Scripture, architecture, and liturgy. But these signs are not meaningful apart from the interpretive process by which they become a part of the life of members.

Josiah Royce has expounded the significance of this process of interpretation in *The Problem of Christianity*.[4] Through the interpretation of its relatively objective signs, the past of the community can become a part of its living present; its memory and its hope can inform its contemporary life. The interpreter must understand the meaning of the sign and he must understand the persons to whom he is interpreting if he is to be effective. The Church is a community of interpretation.

[4] Two vols., New York, 1913.

The signs interpreted mark the differentiation between it and other communities.

Interpretation is a somewhat intellectual process; it can be carried out with some objectivity, and reach the ideational levels of life only. But it may be more subjective in the sense that the interpretation evokes a personal or existential identification with the meanings and signs of the community. Loyalty to the American nation, symbolized in the Declaration of Independence, can be comprehended objectively and viewed with detachment. The interpretation of this sign of the nation's common life, however, may enable one to relive the constituting events of its history, and become subjectively identified with the meaning of these events. A quality of empathetic understanding is employed, in which one understands the meanings as if from within. A reconstruction of these events involves a reliving of them; they become subjectively incorporated into one's personal history.

Wilhelm Dilthey and Max Weber have written about a process called *Verstehen,* subjective understanding. The Christian community is constituted in part by those who have subjectively understood the meanings of its signs. Its members are those for whom an historical event objectively expressed in the Biblical accounts becomes something of a personal event. They are brought together not only out of outward loyalty to certain symbols, but through a shared subjective meaning that the understanding of these symbols evokes. The continuity of the community is not only an outward one of persons who might be counted as having loyalty because they attend divine service, for example. It is an inner continuity of persons through the ages who have understood and relived the same events. The Christian community is a community of subjective understanding; it is a community in which a certain past, delineated by its distinguishing external marks, is relived.

Many persons can relive the constituting events of the Church or the national community through a gift of empathy. Literary genius enables men to participate in the inner experience of other selves or of communities of which they are not members. Thus one cannot simply equate reliving the past with communal membership and participation. There is an added element of loyalty, or self-conscious commitment to a community and its meanings and values. One is a member of a nation partially by accident of birth, and by the processes of communication, interpretation, and understanding (or reliving) its history. But in maturity one acts; one makes a self-conscious commitment of loyalty to the values of the nation. Comparably in the Church, one is a member because one knows its language, participates in the interpretation of its signs, and relives its past. But one also acts, or chooses to become a member.

To some degree, loyalty is born without self-consciousness of the processes that create it. Finally, however, loyalty is commitment; it involves a decision to be identified with the object of loyalty, and to accept certain disciplines consequent upon that decision. Thus the Christian community consists of those who are loyal to Jesus Christ as the constituting person and event of the Christian history. Christians believe in him; they bring life under the interpretation of the meaning of this person. They have an obligation to the community because of this declared loyalty. The Christian Church is a community of loyalty, of faith, of belief. Its object marks its social uniqueness; no other human community self-consciously has Jesus Christ as the center of communal life.

Communal loyalty is expressed in action. Commitment to meanings and values represented in a national symbol is reflected in a way of action, or a sense of mission. Commitment to Jesus Christ, the object of loyalty in the Church, involves the acceptance of a mission, of a purpose which leads to action. The community is not only a community of loyalty; it is a "community of deed," as Royce suggests. The members' sense of identification with it is enhanced by common participation in tasks directed by the central values of the Church. Celebrations in which all members participate are expressions of their loyalty and enhance their identification with one another. The Christian community has many forms of action. Worship, particularly the Lord's Supper, is a common act. Evangelical witness, seeking to bring others to a committed loyalty to Jesus Christ, is Church action. The moral penetration of the other communities to which Christians belong through their vocations is an expression of the community of deed.

In action, loyalty and meaning take outward expression. Action follows self-conscious commitment. Action is directed in part by the purposes that mark the community, in part by the situations in which action takes place. The Church points outwardly from its center of loyalty to action within its own life, and in the wider human community of which it is a part. The Church is a community of deed.

Throughout a social interpretation of the Church runs a double theme. The Church is marked by an inwardness, a common quality of life and commitment to certain truths. It is marked by an outwardness, signs and symbols, books and rites, by which persons of general cultural knowledge can designate it. It is both external and internal; it is outwardly institutional, and inwardly communal. The double character of its life is necessary; the most intimate sense of unity depends upon the outward expressions given to the past life and events remembered in the community. One may choose to designate the point at which he deems given persons to be outside or inside the Church. It may be a mark of relatively external participation, or it may be the mark of an inner loyalty. To make this moral judgment, however, is not an important purpose of a social interpretation of the Church.

The Church shares in common with other communities a natural and political character. The common characteristics, however, do not end here. It shares the processes that make any community identifiable through time and across space. Its differentiation does not lie in the fact that it has a language, but in *its particular language*; it does not lie in the processes of interpretation and subjective understanding, but in that which it interprets and understands. Loyalty and deeds are common to all communities; the specific object of loyalty and its consequent effect upon actions marks the differentiation between the Church and other communities. Thus one moves, in a social theory of the Church, from the common toward the unique. Uniqueness per se is not a quality of the Christian community; its object of loyalty and faith marks its uniqueness.

One does not move from the less theological to the more theological. At every point one might consider the meaning of the social and historical processes in the light of Christian belief about divine action through Jesus Christ and the work of the Holy Spirit. This is a theological task toward which the present essay points, but does not complete. Suffice it to comment: perhaps God acts through the very processes of Church life that can be interpreted from the point of view of social theory.[5]

[5] See D. Bonhoeffer, *Sanctorum Communio, Eine Dogmatische Untersuchung zur Soziologie der Kirche*, Berlin and Frankfort, 1930, p. 179, "Now the objective spirit of the community becomes really the Holy Spirit, the lived experience of the 'religious' community is now really the lived experience of the Church, and the collective person of the Church really 'Christ existing as community.'" This conclusion is similar to that of our Chap. 8, and uses some of the same concepts used in this book. But Bonhoeffer's starting point is virtually opposite of ours, as his subtitle indicates. Cf. p. 70, "Only from the idea of revelation can one come to the idea of the Christian Church." Although there is a special sense i which I agree with this, it clearly is not my basic premise. Also, Bonhoeffer thinks in normative sociological terms. Cf. p. 19, "The basic social category is the I-Thou relation." Thus Bonhoeffer's book does not include most of the issues discussed in this book, e.g., the social continuity of the church, its political character, etc.

CHAPTER 2

The Church:
a Natural Community

The Christian Church is a natural community. This assertion is offensive to some theologians, and to many pastors and laymen. It appears to reduce a special creation of God's gracious work to the dismal and uninspiring realm of natural man with his physical, social, and psychological needs. Insofar as the Church is a natural community it seems to be something less than it is called to be. From a sociological point of view, however, many of the functions that the Church performs are comparable to those of other natural communities, such as the family, the nation, and the social class. Further, life in the Church is comparable to the religious life of non-Christian primitive societies. The Church's rites and beliefs fulfill many of the same natural needs as primitive rites and beliefs.

The same processes of social interaction take place both in the Church and in other human communities.

What is meant by "the Church" in this context? The reference is to the communal life of Christian people wherever and whenever they gather as Christians. Thus it refers to a local congregation, a denomination, or a council of churches. It refers to the sense of being one people that Christians have as a global religious community, even though this community never meets as a whole. Certain human needs can be met at each social level. For example, most human beings need to have their personal values sustained and confirmed by others; they need to participate in a community that has a common outlook on life and the world. Personal values can be nourished in the meeting of a congregation, in a general assembly of a denomination, in a conference meeting for a weekend, or in a meeting of an international Christian group. One person may have this need met better in a small prayer group in a local congregation, another in a mass assembly. The Church fulfills certain needs more adequately in one social form than in another. The need for personal interaction under religious auspices is generally better met in a local group in which relationships are sustained over a long period of time than in a spatially more inclusive group. But wherever the Church is gathered some of man's natural needs are met.

What is meant by natural needs? One answer is simple. Men have certain physical needs that must be fulfilled in a socially acceptable manner. We must have food, shelter, and a basis for mating. The Church obviously does not have the meeting of the physical necessities of Homo sapiens as its primary function, or even as an important function except in times of a social crisis such as a famine. Yet such needs are met in some activities of the Church. More often, however, a religiously acceptable way of meeting these needs is defined. Jewish and Roman Catholic dietary regulations are cases in point. Another is sexual recruitment, which is not a purpose of the Church in any theologically normative definitions. Yet socially acceptable courtship and marriage take place within the Christian community; the marriage is celebrated as an act with religious significance. Man's physical nature is the occasion for certain religious rites and beliefs; it is interpreted and in part governed by his life in the Church. The Christian community meets some physical needs directly, and defines a religiously acceptable way of understanding and meeting others.

Not all natural needs are reducible to the processes of physical self-preservation. Man has psychological and emotional needs; he desires approval and longs for new experiences. He must belong to some socially integrated group if he is to bear the marks of human culture; he must be socialized. The groups to which he belongs have their own "functional requisites"; their continued existence as identifiable human communities depends upon the proper functioning of social processes. Not only the religious group as a society, but the wider society in which the religious group exists must maintain an integrity or balance within the changing values and patterns of life. These non-physical needs are fulfilled in the Church as well as in the family, the school, and the nation. Men find participation in the actions of the Church to be emotionally and psychologically rewarding. The Church, like other societies, is an agent of socialization; persons absorb socially acceptable values within the life of the Christian community. The Church participates in processes common to all human communities as it maintains its social and historical identity; it must have adequate ways to transmit its cultural heritage, or to control aberrant behavior within the community. The Church also is an agent of social integration in the wider society of men; participation in the life of the Church may sustain one's sense of belonging to a nation or a particular social class.

The Church is a natural community. Like all other human groups, one point of reference for its activities is the meeting of various human needs, both individual and social. Any comprehensive social interpretation of the Church must take the human functions of religious group life into account.[1]

The Life of the Body: an occasion for Church life

Man's physical development provides occasions for religious rites and religious interpretation. If religious activity does not fulfill a bodily need directly, it often gives a new meaning to physical life. Functional theorists of religion have long noted the relationship of religious rites and beliefs to significant moments in man's physical life. This is so obvious that it is hardly worth comment; yet it does indicate a natural basis of religious life often scoffed at by theologians. Certain activities of the Church can be interpreted in this framework, as a few examples will reveal.

Cultural anthropologists have shown that primitive societies have initiation rites in which younger members of the clan or tribe are given the secret lore and take on adult responsibilities. These rites normally occur during the age of puberty. In part they celebrate the emergence of physical maturity, in part they are the means for transmitting the esoteric elements of cultural heritage. There are parallel functions in the Church. The rite of confirmation, and the rite of believer's baptism, meet some of the same personal and social needs as primitive initiation rites. Emerging bodily maturity marks growing personal maturity, and both are celebrated in a religious rite. The rites of the Church operate with reference to biological stages of life. Confirmation is the certifica-

[1] There are many interpretations of the basic needs of men by psychologists, sociologists, anthropologists, and philosophers. The outlook of the present chapter has been informed by the writings of Bronislaw Malinowski, and various refinements of his work. Malinowski has distinguished between "basic needs" and "derived needs." Each of the basic needs is met with a cultural response: metabolism with a commissariat, reproduction with a kinship system, bodily comfort with shelter, safety with protection, health with hygiene, etc. At the level of derived needs he finds "imperatives" that are essential for the continued existence of social life, which in turn ultimately rest on basic physical needs. The production of goods is the basis of economic life, the need for peaceful life is the basis of patterns of social control, the transmission of heritage for education, etc. See Malinowski, *A Scientific Theory of Culture*, Chapel Hill, 1944, pp. 91-131. Emile Durkheim laid primary stress on the need for communal integration, and thus one finds a theory of the social functions of religious rites and beliefs in his *Elementary Forms of the Religious Life*, Glencoe, 1954, pp. 205-39, 415-47, and in other essays. Professor Marion J. Levy, Jr. lists ten "functional requisites" for the existence of any society in *The Structure of Society*, Princeton, 1952, pp. 149-97.

tion that the young persons understand the "myths" and "lore" of the Christian community. The junior members have come of age, and are prepared for adult participation in the group. Believer's baptism administered to a young person certifies that he has met the requirements of knowledge, belief, and personal maturity that mark the privilege of full participation in the Church.[2]

Puberty is only one of the physical stages or events given religious significance. Birth, marriage, and death have religious meanings in almost all cultures. The Christian rite of infant baptism obviously does not have the religious sanction and celebration of birth as its normative purpose. But, however its theological intention is defined, the rite has social and personal functions as well. It is comparable to the rite of circumcision in the culture of the people of Israel. Birth is an occasion for joyful celebration, and for an appropriate religious rite that marks the reception of the child into the religious community. Baptism represents the parents' desire for the preservation of the child's good estate through life and beyond death. Birth is an occasion of religious significance.

The religious status of marriage has been debated in the history of the Church. The refusal of Protestants to designate it as a sacrament (as do Catholics) is only one indication of the uncertainty whether marriage is primarily a natural bond, a civil bond, or a religious bond. But most persons in Western society regard it as an occasion of religious significance regardless of the theological debates of the Church. A new status in life, physical and social, is accepted as a time of religious celebration, blessing, and interpretation. It seems "natural" to have a marriage consecrated by a clergyman in a church in Western society.

One famous list of personality needs is W. I. Thomas' four wishes for new experience, for security, for response, and for recognition, cited in much sociological literature, e.g., *Encyclopedia of the Social Sciences*, Vol I, p. 206.

The concept "function" appears in this chapter without technical discussion of its use in the social sciences. The literature in which its adequacy is evaluated is growing. Malinowski's article, "Culture," in the *Encyclopedia of the Social Sciences*, gives an excellent interpretation of culture based on a functional theory. J. Milton Yinger, in *Religion, Society, and the Individual*, New York, 1957, pp. 56-60, develops a functional interpretation of religion. The best critical essay on the concept and its uses is Robert Merton's "Manifest and Latent Functions," in his *Social Theory and Social Structure*, Glencoe, 1949, pp. 21-81.

[2] Malinowski believes that initiation rites among primitive tribes have as their primary function the transmission of cultural heritage; their derived function overshadows the physical occasion. *Magic, Science, and Religion*, Boston and Glencoe, 1948, p. 21. This is obviously the case with Christian rites of confirmation.

Life in marriage begins with at least a dim acknowledgment of a meaning beyond the physical. While a clear understanding of the theological meaning of the rite may escape the clergyman and couple alike, Christian marriage rites give an acceptable celebration of a new physical and social status.

Death, which is from one point of view simply the end of physiological processes in a given organism, seems to be the most significant occasion for religious reflection and rites in all societies. The fact of death raises "religious" questions both for persons who sense its coming, and for those who survive. This physical event with its crucial consequences evokes reflection upon questions of the ultimate significance of existence. Men seek some consolation in a resolution of the questions that are asked about the unknown. The affirmation of personal immortality may represent a natural desire for self-preservation. Or it may meet the need for assurance that one's identity with his group will be maintained; he will gather his family around him on the "other side." In either case the belief in personal immortality can be interpreted as the fulfillment of a natural desire. The occasion of a death evokes religious responses. Families turn to the Church for consolation, and for an affirmation of the rightness of all things in spite of their disruption. The Church provides such consolation. It meets a natural need.

To claim that the Church's celebration of Holy Communion meets man's need for physical sustenance in any substantial way is patently absurd. Yet its religious meaning cannot be understood without reference to the normal physical functions of eating and drinking. Simple physical elements, bread and wine, have a sophisticated religious meaning in the rite. In the physical acts of eating and drinking the believer partakes of divine grace. The precise relationship of the physical substances of bread and wine to the presence of Christ is, of course, subject to continuing debate. Yet eating and drinking, basic physical actions, are interpreted to mean the partaking of the body and blood of Christ. Physical actions are the occasion for religious experience and interpretation.

Whether rites and beliefs are *caused* by physical needs and secondary ones derived therefrom, or whether the physical events simply provide *the occasion* for Christian interpretation and Church actions, cannot easily be determined. Normatively for the Church, the latter would be the case. Empirically for many members of the Church, the former might be the case. National folk churches as well as American denominations recognize that many persons avail themselves of the ministry of the Church for baptism of infants, confirmation of young people, the consecration of marriages, and funerals. This has importance for a social interpretation of the Church; it may indicate that a functional interpretation of Church life, referring to the basic physical events of life, has a significant measure of adequacy.

The Needs of Personality: an occasion for Church life[3]

Various needs of the human personality are met by participation in Church life, as well as in other social groups. Political parties, business corporations, secret societies, trade unions, and other voluntary associations all have psychological and emotional rewards for their members. The Church, like other communities, functions with reference to these human needs. The motivations for participating in the life of the Church are at least as varied and complex as the motivations for belonging to any other group. This is to say that the psychological functions of the Church for both laymen and clergy are as varied and complex as the psychological functions of other groups.

The profession of the ministry provides various personal satisfactions. The minister may hold public respect by virtue of his office. Through his personal relations and preaching he may have an important influence on persons and their decisions and actions. For his achievements he may be admired and even adulated. He may find a satisfactory opportunity to develop talents for administration and leadership. If he is intellectually inclined, the ministry offers some opportunities for a continued life of study. Membership in the profession brings opportunities to travel and to meet persons of importance in the ecclesiastical world. The minister may enjoy the isolation from the competitive struggles of society that his office sometimes ensures. He may become the public symbol of a pure morality, or of a peace and serenity that life does not afford to others. Or the office may lead him into the struggles and suffering of men; he may have the personal reward of seeing suffering assuaged or reconciliation achieved as the fruit of his efforts. For the man of prophetic or critical temperament the Church provides a

---

[3] Any adequate development of this topic would require a review of the total literature in the psychology of religion. In this chapter the intention is only to show that life in the Church meets needs of men that are not particularly religious in their primary character. This section merely illustrates that thesis. For a summary of work in this field see W. H. Clark, *Psychology of Religion*, New York, 1959.

place in which he can stand over against the forces of evil. He can question the moral rectitude of the world in the light of the Church's beliefs. Participation in controversy within the Church and its social milieu may be no less rewarding than being the public symbol of other-worldliness.

To be sure, the ministry creates personal conflicts and tensions as well. The minister's normative conception of his task may differ from that of his congregation; in a particular situation this contrast may become serious. The tension that he feels because of the conflicting claims of his congregation, his denomination, the wider community, and his family may create suffering. He may be uncertain in a given situation about what he ought to do and why he ought to do it, and thus experience anxiety. These dilemmas only illustrate some of the tensions in which a minister may find himself. To cite them, however, is not to imply that they are stronger than the rewards. Further, both rewards and anxieties may be related not only to the objective situation, and to levels of self-understanding that a minister can articulate, but also to deeper sources of motivation that lie below the threshold of consciousness. Participation in the Church has important psychological functions for the minister, just as any other vocation has for those who are engaged in it.

The personal functions of Church life for the layman are at least as complex as those for the ministry. It may give one a "lift," that is, raise the level of his morale. Worship may be a meaningful escape from the stresses and strains of life; it may bring serenity and certainty in the midst of ambiguity. Religious beliefs may provide the framework in which the devout interpret human crises to their own emotional satisfaction. Various talents can be used in the service of the Church, whether in a congregation or some other gathering of Christian people. The Church, like other social organizations, gives opportunities to exercise leadership potential, musical talent, administrative acumen, and many more gifts. Lay leadership in the Church has rewards comparable to those that come from participation in other voluntary associations.

The meetings of congregations or other Christian groups may provide what some now call "a community of acceptance." Here a person may be trusted as a pure "I," without reference to his social status or moral merit. Here another may be met as a pure "thou," without concern for the social roles and symbols through which interaction normally takes place. More likely the experience is less free from the outside patterns of life than is generally assumed. A meeting of Christians may provide a religious reinforcement for the assumption that "our kind of people" are God's kind of people. Values of a particular portion of the society may be sustained and given religious sanction. Patterns of behavior characteristic of a particular social and religious group, such as rural American evangelical Protestantism, may become more entrenched under the impact of a consensus among the believers. Men may become religiously certain that all they do and think is absolutely right.

In any or all of its emotional and psychological functions the Church resembles other groups. It bears the marks of a natural community, providing fulfillment of desires and needs that are common to all men. In it men receive recognition; they have a sense of belonging; they may be assured of the ultimate rightness and goodness of things. Even the suppressed drives of life may find socially acceptable outlets and religious sanction. One cannot conceive of a single form of Church life that has no emotional and psychological functions.

The Need for Social Integration

The Church sustains the integration of human societies. To be sure, churches often are factors in social differentiation and tension, e.g., in Catholic-Protestant strife or in anti-Semitism. This must be acknowledged. In both its integrating and differentiating functions, however, the Church resembles the other communities of man. The nation-state functions integratively with reference to one portion of human society —its own members. It also functions to differentiate the total human community; in this regard it may become socially disintegrative. Trade unions, political parties, and even organizations formed to unite all men in peace and goodwill all have the same double function. To acknowledge that the Church often is a factor in the cleavages in human society does not vitiate the fact that it also has an integrative function. What functions with reference to one group as integrative may be disintegrative in relation to a wider group.

The socially integrative function of religion is commonly noted by social scientists and theologians. It can be observed in many societies. For example, in some African and Asian societies, Islam, with the Koran as a source of law and ethics, dominates the culture. Both the common mores of the people and the legislation of their governments are impregnated by this religion. Also in culturally isolated primitive societies the religious community is often coextensive with the tribe, the clan, or the family. Thus the unity of a society is reinforced by religious beliefs and rites.[4]

The Church has not always been integrative, partly because some Christians do not believe that this is its proper function. Christians sometimes believe that the Church is called to be set apart from, or even over against, the natural communities of men. Groups that withdraw from the world often recall the words of Jesus, "And brother will deliver up brother to death, and the father his child, and children will rise against parents and have them put to death; and you will be hated by all for my name's sake." (Mark 13:12-13, designated by scholars as an apocalyptic passage.) This implies for some Christians that their community is so unique in its loyalty that it disrupts all the natural communities of men, including the family. Sectarian movements and reforms have often arisen in the history of the Church as protests against the excessive identification of the Church with a particular culture or nation. Such protests imply a criticism of the assumption that social integration is a proper function of the Church.

Whether or not it is normatively proper, however, the Church has functioned as an integrating agent. In the history of pre-Reformation Europe, for example, the unity of Western culture was intertwined with the catholicity of the Church. Art, literature, civic festivals, and morality were all informed by the apparent unity of the basic principles of the Church and society. Ernst Troeltsch was so impressed by the evidence of this unity that he defined his ideal-type of the Church in its light. The Church-type of religious organization is characterized in part by the coextensiveness of the Christian community with the cultural community. The great age of its historical manifestation was the medieval period, with its Christendom.[5] The thesis that Western Culture would not have had its characteristic unity apart from the exist-

[4] The totemistic interpretation of primitive religion made by Durkheim stresses its integrative function. Religious signs and symbols, such as the totem image of the tribe, function as collective representations of the collective consciousness of the group. See his *Elementary Forms of the Religious Life,* pp. 205-39. Yinger and Joachim Wach also discuss this function. See, e.g., Wach, *Sociology of Religion,* Chicago, 1944, pp. 34 ff. and Yinger, *op. cit.,* pp. 60-72.

[5] See Troeltsch, *The Social Teachings of the Christian Churches,* Vol. I, Glencoe and New York, 1949, pp. 331-43, for the contrast of Church and sect-types. Many points of his differentiation are germane to this discussion. The Church-type of Christendom exists as a hope to be actualized for some of our contemporaries. The social thought of Christopher Dawson, V. A. Demant, J. Maritain, and T. S. Eliot particularly point toward this hope.

ence of the Church is widely accepted, though difficult to substantiate with precision. The Christian community with its penetration of almost every aspect of the culture has functioned as an integrating force.

The "national church" as it is embodied in the Church of England and the Scandinavian churches manifests the integrative function of the Christian community. Where national citizenship and church membership have been virtually one, as particularly in Scandinavia, religion sustains national unity. Until the sectarianism of the past eighty years, for example, to be a Swede was to be a Lutheran. The parish system— in which the church is responsible for some of the functions of a clerk of the state—is a remnant of a time when the integration had more meaning than it now does. At the parish level the religious-social unity of the nation had its strong local counterpart. One's local place of identification was his parish. Certain rites and services of national churches still symbolize the religious reinforcement of national self-consciousness. The coronation of the British monarch by the Archbishop of Canterbury with all its pomp and splendor points to the mutual strengthening of church and national life. The religious service of Christmas matins in Sweden is virtually a national folk rite: the celebration of Swedishness and of the birth of Christ become one.

In the pluralistic American society the religiosity that sustains national unity stems from no particular church. Indeed, since many citizens are of Jewish faith and background, it takes a form that is not specifically Christian. A more inclusive and vague religious loyalty, "faith in faith," to which many churches and religious groups contribute, is believed to be a source of national strength and unity.[6] How deeply American people believe that religious faith strengthens the national life is difficult to ascertain. It is clear, however, that political and other national leaders assume that religion strengthens social unity, for most civic occasions find an invocation of the deity to be appropriate.

The Church often reinforces the self-consciousness of a social class. Ample evidence has been gathered to show a significant correlation between social classes and particular denominations in the United States, and in particular congregations in towns and cities. The support that religion gives to the integrity and interest of a social class is often subtle, and sometimes crude. There is some evidence for the Marxist

[6] Will Herberg in *Protestant-Catholic-Jew*, New York, 1955, describes the social significance of the three faiths, and in the last chapter subjects the general American religiosity to severe criticism. See pp. 270-89.

charge that the Church has provided an ideology for the claims of economic interests. Sidney Mead has shown that the Protestant churches of the United States in the nineteenth century were careful to delineate between the spheres of power of Church and state, but were not concerned about the full support that religion was giving to the ideology of the expanding business community. He cites many statements from the popular religious literature of the period. The Reverend Francis Wayland, president of Brown University and a leading Baptist minister, declared with reference to the growth of the American economy,

What nation will be second in the new order of things, is yet to be decided; but the providence of God has already announced, that if true to ourselves, we shall be inevitably first.[7]

Bishop Lawrence of Massachusetts, Horace Bushnell of Hartford, and Henry Ward Beecher of Brooklyn were all quite certain that riches and godliness were the warp and woof of the good life. Movements continue to exist which seek to show that the true life and faith of the Christian community is the best sustainer of *laissez-faire* capitalism. Some of those who make this claim believe that they are concerned for the total national interest, and not that of a particular class, though the economy they would revive is certain to be particularly beneficial to owners and managers.

The moral protest by Christian reformers against the power of the entrepreneurs tended to identify the right life and practice of the Christian community with the economic and social aspirations of the industrial workers. Their intention was not so much to reinforce a special class interest as to show the social justice of labor's struggle. Not all religious identification with the disinherited, however, has been in the name of social reform. Religion has functioned as an opiate of the downtrodden. Pentecostal and holiness sects thrive among those who do not have many of the rewards of prosperity. The intention of the revival preacher is never to create a class-consciousness in an economic group. A satisfactory adjustment to adverse conditions, however, has often been an unintended consequence (a latent function, in Robert Merton's terms) of church life. The communal life of Christian groups

[7] Cited by Sidney Mead in "American Protestantism since the Civil War. I. From Denominationalism to Americanism." *Journal of Religion*, Vol. 36 (1956), p. 11.

makes existence tolerable for men in a social status over which they have limited control.[8]

The integrative function of the Church takes on a new character in the contemporary urbanized, mobile society in the United States. Where identification with any local tradition is broken by social mobility, the Church often functions as a "home away from home." The congregation becomes a place where a stranger can meet "like-minded people," and find social acceptance and participation. The Church is often the door through which one finds his social friends in the American suburb. Anonymity of urban existence with the consequent breakdown of old patterns of social control are overcome in part by identification with the Church. The notion dominant in American Protestantism that the urban congregation ought to be shaped by the image of the socially homogeneous rural congregation of a more stable society indicates the extent to which the function of social integration is accepted.

Other evidence of the integrative function of the Church both in practice and in the normative declaration of its role can be cited. For example, the popular dictum "Families that pray together stay together," as it is repeated in Protestant as well as in Roman Catholic circles, indicates the wide acceptance of this function as both actual and normative. The importance of the Church to the American Negro population, both in Northern cities and in the South, can be interpreted through various specifications of the theme of social integration.[9] The political unity of Western Europe, it has been suggested, will rest finally upon the acceptance of classical notions of natural law as they have been incorporated into the theology and moral life of the Roman Catholic community. All of the evidence suggests that the function of social integration is part of the significance of the Church, whether it is normatively accepted or not. The Church is a natural community; like other groups and institutions, its beliefs, common life, and practices often sustain the unity and harmony of various human societies.

[8] For evidence of this see, e.g., Liston Pope's *Millhands and Preachers,* New Haven, 1942, especially pp. 133-40. The literature on the relation of religion to social class is growing. In addition to many American studies, European studies have been made, e.g., Berndt Gustafsson's *Kyrkoliv och Samhällsklass,* Stockholm, 1950, and E. R. Wickham, *Church and People in an Industrial City,* London, 1957.
[9] See, e.g., St. Clair Drake and Horace Cayton, *Black Metropolis,* New York, 1945, pp. 422 ff., 611 ff., and 670 ff.

The Need for Institutional Self-preservation

The Church, like other particular historical communities, seeks to continue its existence in time. Certain "functional requisites" must be adequately met if the identity of a particular society is to persist. The Church, in common with other groups, must have adequate procedures to preserve itself.[10] For example, it must socialize its members around its particular meanings and patterns of life; its beliefs and purposes must be transmitted from one generation to another. If it is to maintain its identity as a particular community it must cultivate a "shared cognitive orientation," a pattern of meanings and values that marks the outlooks of its members. The institutions of the Church, like others, must have certain sanctions by which they exercise control in the achievement of goals and fulfillment of purposes. Self-preservation is not the only motive for this; the possibility of executing its theologically defined mission and purpose depends upon the Church fulfilling these natural functions.

From New Testament times to the present the Church has given much attention to the processes of socialization. It is concerned that its converts be properly identified with its differentium before they are formally received into membership. Birthright members are guided and instructed prior to their acceptance as mature participants. The activities of catechetical instruction and Sunday Schools, preaching and evangelization, all function to transmit a pattern of beliefs and values in order to maintain the social identity and unity of the Church. Historical continuity depends upon the functioning of the same socialization processes that other communities use. Since an imperative of the Church's belief requires it to be concerned for the welfare of the whole of mankind, the religious socialization processes extend into the wider social and cultural milieu as well. The Church believes that it must bring its message and life to all men. Thus the saving of the nations, if not their proper governing, demands an extension of the Church's socialization activities. Conviction of the truth of this mission in turn strengthens the identity and unity of the Church, for the natural processes of teaching become normative tasks.

The Church, like other human groups, is identified by its outlook on the world. There must be some consensus regarding the basic perspective from which life is to be viewed and lived. This "shared cognitive

[10] See Marion J. Levy, Jr., *op. cit.* In this section I use three of Levy's ten concepts.

orientation" is not a method of study, as it is in the scientific community. Rather it is a set of convictions that are believed to be important, and worthy of the attention of all men. These convictions may subtly shade and color the way in which Christians think and live rather than be a set of prescriptive propositions applicable to life. The convictions of the Church function more like the democratic faith of the American people than they do like the scientific method or a code of rules. Tyranny, for example, is bad to most Americans not because it violates a principle that they can repeat, but because it is offensive to the moral consensus of the nation. The Christian community as a whole depends for its identity, that is, its differentiation from other human groups, on a shared cognitive orientation.

Particular groups within the history of the Church have their specified ways of understanding reality. Particular churches are characterized by particular orientations of conviction and life. Lutherans presumably understand one another better than they understand non-Lutherans within the Church. Certain ideas and patterns of life have been transmitted through the Lutheran community that are more or less distinctive to it. One function of such characteristic Lutheran concepts as law and gospel, and *simul justus et peccator*, is to give social identity to an historical community. Other groups within the Church have their special concepts and patterns of life. Just as Russians are distinguished from Brazilians, and Buddhists from Moslems, by "shared cognitive orientations," so are various groups within the Christian community.

The Church, like other human groups, has sanctions that are used in determining its goals and the proper means for achieving them. There must be some basis for judging the rightness of action and belief in all human groups. This is as true for thieves as for anyone else, as the old adage reminds us. In this respect as well, the Church is a natural community. Theologians, pastors, and teachers help to determine and interpret the sanctions. Synods and boards of deacons function as courts of judgment in control of the "power of the keys" to the human Church, if not to heaven. Particular groups of Christians invoke particular sanctions, and exercise their control over goals and means in different ways. In some the ordination to the priesthood marks great power and privilege; in others the majority vote of laymen is determinative. In some formal trials for heresy occur; in others the pressures toward exclusion may be more subtle but no less effective. The seat of authority to determine proper action rests in different places, as does the power to control marginal or aberrant behavior. Yet every congregation, denomination, or council of churches, as a natural community, must have sanctions and the power to use them. The composite effect gives social shape to the whole Church.

The naturalness of the Christian community may be so obvious that it is ignored. The theologians have been so interested in finding the differentiating and unique elements in the Church that they have generally overlooked the qualities and patterns of its life that are continuous with other societies. Given their focus of attention, it is often tacitly assumed that the natural basis of the Church is unimportant. Or it appears to be assumed that the religious significance of the natural elements in the Church's life is so unique as to transform them into something discontinuous with other human groups. In the development of a social interpretation of the Church, however, one notes the importance of the natural aspects of the Church: the meeting of individual and social needs. These are ingredients in the life of the Church without which it could not exist. The Church is in one dimension a natural community, and can be understood in the light of the same principles used to interpret other natural communities— the family, non-Christian primitive religions, the nation, or the trade union. The processes of its life are not unique, as further specification shows.

CHAPTER 3

The Church:
a Political Community

The Christian Church is a political community. This fact is very difficult for many Christians, and particularly American Protestants, to accept. The Church presumably ought to be "above politics," to find ways of work that do not involve the use of institutional and personal power. It ought to be a "truly spiritual" community.

If the political aspects of Church life are recognized, they are often suppressed from open acknowledgment. They may be tolerated, or relegated to the realm of "administration" without affirmation of their necessity and usefulness in the common life. Some theologians see the political life of the Church as one of the marks of its fall, or at least its earthly imperfection. Emil Brunner, for example, interprets the true community of Christians to exist in I-Thou relationships which are a gift of grace. Institutionalization is at best a stifling necessity. Political institutionalization is less true to the essence of Christian community than some other forms of its persisting patterns of life.[1] This point of view is representative of the spiritualizing tendencies of many Protestants.

The relation of the political processes in the Church to its character as a more "spiritual" fellowship is difficult to describe precisely. It is somewhat comparable to the relation between the state as an institution and the nation as a gathering of people. In one sense the nation is prior in time and importance; it represents the living values and beliefs, the ways of work and life that exist. However, for this life to be ordered, some form of political authority embodied in the state must be accepted. This political order at its best is the appropriate expression of the fundamental characteristics of the nation's culture.

In another sense, however, the state is prior. It uses its power and authority to direct and preserve the basic cultural faith of the nation. The continued existence of the nation is dependent upon the exercise of appropriate forms of institutional power. For example, the basic democratic faith of the American nation cannot be identified simply with its representational form of government. Yet one cannot conceive of the preservation of this democratic faith without its embodiment in representative government. The democratic ethos had to be made formal in the charters and documents of the nation, e.g., the Declaration of Independence and the Constitution. The form of government appropriate to the ethos and its charter needs power to insure the preservation of these values. Thus the system of legislative, executive, and judiciary branches of government is a political necessity for the nation's health.

In a comparable way the existence of the Church as a personal community with its own ethos requires that life be maintained and extended

---

[1] Brunner develops his anti-institutional point of view in *The Misunderstanding of the Church*, Philadelphia, 1953. His fascination with the "no-Church" Christian movement in Japan is an expression of this bias. Rudolph Sohm's interpretation of early Church history reflects this theme. See J. L. Adams' essay, "Rudolph Sohm's Theology of Law and the Spirit," in W. Leibrecht (ed.), *Religion and Culture*, New York, 1959, pp. 219-35.

through the definition and use of appropriate political forms. The Church's nature is not exclusively personal, or transpersonal in some spiritual sense. The possibility of the Church being a personal community and maintaining its identity through history rests upon the existence of patterns of authority and power. The exercise of social power is necessary to keep alive the spirit of the community. The fulfillment of the mission of the Church requires the development of political processes and the use of social power. As the relationship between the nation and the state is reciprocal, so also is that between the Church as a personal (or interpersonal) community, and the Church as a political order.

Much discussion of "church order" ignores the sphere of politics. The question debated most often is whether a general organizational plan is appropriate to certain Biblical texts or theological doctrines. Is a congregational order more authentic according to the criteria of the true nature of the Church than an episcopal or presbyterian order? The relation of formal constitutional patterns of organization to theological criteria is the focus of attention. If one faces the life of the Church from this point of view exclusively, however, the political structures, functions, and dynamics of the Church are poorly understood. Theologians often fail to account for the distribution of political power in the Church. In a social interpretation of the Church it is more appropriate to examine the actual processes taking place than to exegete Biblical texts, or speculate on the appropriateness of the three classical forms of church order. The Church in its working life is a political community.

A Working Definition of Politics in the Church

The interpretation of the Church as a political community focuses on its patterns of life as an "institution." The definitions of "institution" vary. Some theologians prefer to reserve the word to indicate orders or patterns of life "instituted" by God. Sociological definitions are numerous. An acceptable definition for present purposes is as follows: An institution is a relatively persistent pattern of action or relationships in human society.[2] A social structure can be understood in both its persistence and its changes. An institution is related to its own time and place; it is dynamic and functional. Yet it is more permanent

[2] Cf. Levy, *The Structure of Society*, pp. 101-9; he defines institution as "a particular type of normative pattern that affects human action in terms of a social system," p. 102.

than a single action or temporary relationship; it is a pattern through which actions take place.

The political structure of the Church then is *the patterns of relationships and action through which policy is determined and social power exercised.* As a human society the Church must determine policy, and it must have the necessary social power to act in the light of its decisions. It defines its nature and task; it develops the means needed to achieve its mission in the world; it finds the necessary forms of social power to achieve some of its goals. Patterns exist through which authority is granted or assumed by particular persons in order to perform particular duties. Often power is exercised in churches without formal authorization. Where the authorization is clear, the persons chosen for positions come to office through political processes. During their tenure of office, officials are subject to the pressures of the public opinion of their constituencies and of other persons and groups.

In all these respects the Church is comparable in its life to political parties, business organizations, trade unions, the state, and various voluntary organizations. The concepts and language of the analysts of power in government shed light on the use of power in the churches. The ideas developed by the students of bureaucracy in modern society aid in the understanding of the procedures of churches. The problems of the responsible use of power exist across the lines between Church and State and all other institutions of society. All of this, which is so striking to persons engaged in the life of a congregation, denomination, or ecumenical agency, seems to escape the attention of most contemporary writers on the nature of the Church.[3]

The Pervasiveness of Church Politics

Political life pervades every particular organizational form of the Church. Its patterns differ in different traditions and denominations. The moderator of a Presbyterian General Assembly in the United States is elected by the messengers to the annual meeting of that body.

[3] Two recent dissertations in the Yale University Graduate School have explored Church politics and bureaucracy in a highly illuminating way. One is a study of the American Baptist Convention, by Paul M. Harrison, Princeton University, and the other is "The Methodist Board of Temperance, A Study in Church Policy Making," by Joseph L. Allen, Perkins School of Theology. Harrison's conceptual framework is adapted from bureaucracy studies; Allen's from political science. I am indebted to these men for their research which substantiates many impressions reflected in this chapter. Harrison's has been published under the title *Authority and Power in the Free Church Tradition*, Princeton, 1959.

The Pope of the Roman Catholic Church is elected by the College of Cardinals. The business committee of an American Congregational church is elected at its annual business meeting. A bishop in the Church of Sweden is chosen by the government from among three candidates elected by the clergy of the diocese. In each instance one can safely surmise that the political processes do not begin and end with the formal balloting. Interested parties evaluate potential candidates in the light of their qualifications and the particular requirements of the office for the period of tenure involved. Candidates must be weighed in the light of the potential support or hostility of various interest groups in the churches. Informal discussions take place in which groups come to some consensus about supporting particular candidates. And it is not unknown for a candidate to campaign in ways comparable to those adopted by a man seeking nomination to an office in government.

A pastor desires laymen on his various committees and boards to be in general sympathy with his understanding of the mission of the Church. If he believes that stewardship education is important, he will exercise his influence to have officers selected who have an interest and ability in that work. If a congregation is to raise funds to construct a new building, persons with particular abilities will be chosen for the appropriate positions. Ministers have powers of recommendation, if not selection; they often work closely with the nominating committees of their congregations; and many are adept at "sounding out" persons of power regarding their support in potentially controversial matters.

A denominational executive's actions may follow a similar political pattern. He will seek to have staff colleagues appointed who share his convictions about the purpose of the Church and the tasks to be done. If he believes, for example, that mass evangelism is the best technique for advancing the cause of the Church, he will exercise his influence (i.e., astutely use political means) to have a staff person of like conviction appointed to a position of evangelistic responsibility. Ecumenical organizations are not exempt from political processes common to congregations and denominations. At every social level both personal influence and authorized political machinery are at work to keep the churches moving, and often in a direction set by persons already in power.

Yet at every level the political activity must be carried on with an ear to the constituency. Popes and bishops, executive secretaries and board members, pastors and deacons, must be aware of various points of view and interests that are represented in the churches. Ecumenical agencies keep the special concerns of particular denominations in an effective state of balance. No official in the churches at any level can afford to alienate the major body of those who have elected him to ecclesiastical power.[4]

The Dynamics of Church Politics

Politics in the Church or in the state is a process and not a static pattern. To understand the politics one must look at the process by which decisions are made and actions taken. Some of the considerations that are weighed in this process can be noted.

The political process takes place through both the *formal*, established patterns of an organization, and the *informal*, often unauthorized patterns. Students of government, of business, and of voluntary associations have found the co-existence of both patterns in almost every organization in American society, and there is no reason to think that it is limited to the Western Hemisphere. The use of informal patterns sometimes by-passes the formal, sometimes it speeds up the processes within the formal. In many instances the informal structure appears to exercise more power than the duly authorized formal patterns. The formal structures are defined by constitutions, by-laws, tables of organization, and job descriptions. The informal are undefined but real, and are constituted by personal relations and the exercise of personal influence.

Informal patterns often function out of necessity; the formal patterns are inadequate and too cumbersome to meet the needs for which they were created. The General Conference of the Methodist Church, for example, is the legislative authority for a national denomination with approximately ten million members. It meets every four years for two weeks. It is patently clear that this formal structure is in itself inadequate to make the decisions and authorize the actions required by the denomination. Some of the difficulty is met by the authorized

[4] Three brief essays have recently called attention to the importance of political activity in the Church and to some of the consequences forthcoming from not recognizing it: George Forell, "Make Church Politics Ethical," *The Christian Century*, Vol. 70 (1953), pp. 317-18; Charles Page, "Bureaucracy and the Liberal Church," *Review of Religion*, Vol. 16 (1952-53), pp. 139-50; and Walter Muelder, "Institutional Factors Affecting Unity and Disunity," *Ecumenical Review*, Vol. 8 (1956), pp. 113-36. Among social scientists whose studies shed light on the Church are Max Weber, Robert Merton, Peter Blau, Chester Barnard, Paul Appleby, Robert Michels, and Harold Lasswell. Many significant essays can be found in *Reader in Bureaucracy*, ed. Robert Merton, *et al.*, Glencoe, 1952.

delegation of power to boards and agencies. With reference to the legislative process alone, however, a large body meeting as seldom and as briefly as the General Conference cannot possibly fulfill its obligations as an initiating body. It becomes, like most national church legislative bodies, an organ for the approval of proposals thoroughly prepared in advance by both authorized and informal procedures, and a place to promote the interests of various ecclesiastical agencies. Informal structures for policy making are a functional necessity when the formal structures are inadequate.

A problem posed for the churches as well as other organizations is how to keep the informal processes responsible to the proper constituencies. Churches are in highly fluid situations in which power must be exercised with speed, and often without specific authorization. Church officials are sensitive to the need for efficiency in procedures. Perhaps in some instances the official, out of carelessness or other motives, may neglect to exercise his power within the formally defined bounds.

Both the formal and informal systems are changeable. The classical three types of church order—congregational, presbyterian, and episcopal—have all in fact undergone changes in their functions. The conditions of a rationalized industrial society have imposed their own influences on the actual processes of church politics. This is to say that the *functioning* church order is often more flexible in form and action than formal structures lead one to believe. Flexibility is a functional necessity because the policy deliberations and actions of churches have many points of reference; they are not governed by any one simple norm. Like other political decisions, Church decisions stem from many motives and have many ends in view. Changes in the various points of reference require changes in the political processes of Church life.

Normatively, the two most significant points of reference are the definition of the mission and purpose of the Church, and the order of life and culture within which the churches seek to act. Presumably politics in the Church is an instrument of purpose and mission. The system of beliefs is the source of the basic governing principles both for the organization of its political life, and its activities. The political organization and activity exist to be a means through which a defined mission and purpose can be achieved. If the political life of the churches is instrumental in character it is not inherently sacred. It cannot be a pure expression of a doctrine of the Church. As an instrument its adequacy is measured with reference not only to theologically defined purposes but also to the effectiveness of particular ways of work in particular societies and historical periods.

Since both the definition of specific tasks and the situations in which they will be done undergo change, the political forms and activities of the Church remain flexible. The claim that a particular political structure or process is of absolute value may in the long run ossify it. It may become a vestigial form without function, like many church vestments. A political pattern that appears to be grounded in a Biblical or doctrinal image may not be effective as an instrument of the Church's purpose in modern society. This is to say that a social pattern that is functional with reference to the preservation of a certain idea of the Church may not be functional with reference to the conditions within which the Church must work in a particular society. For example, a tentmaker wandering from city to city obviously is no model for a modern board of missions. On the other hand, a pattern that is governed solely by immediate effectiveness in the realization of institutional goals may be inadequate or disfunctional with reference to normatively defined purposes of the Church. For example, effective public relations techniques may increase church membership at the cost of the loss of church discipline. Normative judgments about the adequacy of ecclesiastical political patterns must be made with reference to several criteria.

The historical development of organizations to sustain the missions of the Church on the American Western frontier and in foreign lands illustrates this multiple reference of political organization and process.[5] Under the impact of the revivals and other factors in the early nineteenth century, there was a new stress on one purpose of the Church, namely, evangelism. The conversion of the settlers in the West and the heathen in other lands was a task that caught the imagination and enthusiasm of the established Eastern churches. In most instances, e.g., the Congregational churches, the existing structures of denominational life were inadequate to pursue this mission. Voluntary associations outside of the established ecclesiastical patterns were formed, drawing their membership and contributions from various congregations and denominations. An example is the American Board of Commissioners

[5] I am indebted to Earl MacCormac, of Davidson College, for research presented in his Yale Ph.D. dissertation, 1960, "The Transition from Voluntary Missionary Society to the Church as a Missionary Organization among American Congregationalists, Presbyterians, and Methodists."

for Foreign Missions. For some decades the voluntary missionary society appeared to be an adequate social organization to realize the evangelical task.

As the mission work became widespread and the complexity of the societies grew, however, a new rational ordering of the political process was necessary. Greater efficiency was needed in the gathering of contributions and the enlistment of personnel. Competition among societies, both for resources in the home churches and for converts in the mission fields, was a hindrance to the work. The relationship of numerous voluntary societies to the existing ecclesiastical institutions had to be regularized. Out of these and other needs the patterns for fostering missions changed. Some societies became official boards of denominations. Some united in order to avoid duplication of effort and achieve a rational division of labor. In the course of decades large "holding companies" came into being, such as the Congregational Board of Home Missions, in which some of the autonomy of the societies is maintained within an efficiently organized general administration. New patterns of political representation developed; rather than hold separate meetings of various societies, the same delegates from churches legislate for all the societies. In recent decades new purposes of the Church have been defined because of new social situations, e.g., the concern for the inner-city. New institutional forms emerge, like the East Harlem Protestant Parish in New York City, sponsored partly by regular ecclesisatical organizations and partly by new voluntary associations.

Through the history of the missionary movement in the past century and a half one sees how political forms and processes function with reference to a variety of purposes and needs, and remain flexible in form. The modern rationalization of institutional forms for the purpose of efficiency in industry, unions, and elsewhere, is also taken up into Church life. Churches must find the patterns that are effective in their own time. Specific purposes require new institutional forms; the political life and structure of the churches is instrumental; it is functional and therefore changes.

A contemporary example of the Church seeking the adequate political form for a defined purpose is the ecumenical movement. Indeed, the lack of consensus about the purpose of the movement is one of the difficulties in finding an appropriate political form. If the emphasis is on co-operation among existing denominations, the sprawling bureaucracy of the National Council of the Churches of Christ in the United States of America appears to be the most feasible social form. The main lines of representation are between the denominations and the National Council. One result is a political organization acutely aware of the need for proportionate representation of viewpoints and personnel on various committees, agencies, and in the staff.

If, on the other hand, the stress of ecumenical purpose is to actualize a maximum amount of the "unity" of the Church, another institutional form and function is required. The World Council of Churches takes its institutional shape in part because of the concerns out of which it grew, as these were embodied in the Faith and Order movement and the Life and Work movement. The problems dealt with in these movements grew largely out of theological discussion, and consequently both the World Council's staff and its nonstaff participating elite were drawn heavily from faculties of theology and other intellectuals in the Church. Changing institutionalization can be observed in the World Council of Churches. For example, Faith and Order work, primarily concerned for the question of the unity of the Church, has been relegated to the subordinate position of a Department in the Division of Studies, and has one professional staff person. Other work more immediately functional with reference to less controversial purposes of denominations such as the youth program, and thus more readily suppported with the requisite financial assistance, overshadows Faith and Order in institutional resources. In spite of the direction of institutionalization in the World Council, however, the participation of intellectuals in its work remains high. In the National Council of Churches, in which co-operative action appears to be the functioning purpose, the staff and participants more often represent those who are responsible for programs and administration in the denominations. The recruitment of personnel is often from within the groups with bureaucratic experience, and thus from among those who to some extent may have made their peace and become "bureaucratic personalities." The next decades may show a similar process in the World Council.[6]

An important differentiating factor between the National and World Councils is the geographical scope within which each seeks to be effective. The National Council is confined in most of its work to the rationalized industrial society of the United States, and finds a pattern that is congenial to the types of social organization that are dominant in its milieu. The World Council keeps in view the younger churches in

[6] Robert Merton's discussions of the "bureaucratic personality" and the problems of the intellectual in a bureaucracy are very useful in interpreting churches. See *Social Theory and Social Structure*, pp. 151-78.

the industrially less advanced countries in which Christians are minority groups. Its social organization must be appropriate to effective decision-making and action in the heterogeneous societies of India, Germany, Greece, Africa, and other parts of the world. The pattern of ecumenical institutions will change as purposes are revised and specified, as the ways of work absorb the cultural and social milieus in which they are set, and as the semiautonomous processes of institutionalization inherent in all large-scale social organization have their impact.

A study of the informal political systems within stated tables of organization and traditional polities is likely to reveal as much similarity as diversity in church politics. The power of prestige among both laity and clergy is similar in congregational and episcopal churches. The factors that make for prestige and influence are similar. For example, the pastors of large churches are more influential than the pastors of small churches. The prestige and status of a layman in the Church are often more dependent on his social status than on any distinctively religious criteria. All churches are susceptible to the power of "charismatic authority," i.e., to the dynamic and persuasive influence of gifted personalities. The informal processes by which the first and sometimes final stages of policy-making are reached may consist of luncheons among persons of relatively the same status within the church. The assessment of opposition to an innovation in policy is comparable to the same process in every social organization. The ecclesiastical "organization man" who is acutely sensitive to the winds of favorable opinion, and who knows how to manipulate situations skillfully for the advantage of institutional success (and incidentally his own), is not restricted to one traditional type of polity. Procedures by which formal and informal promises of support are secured for a policy coming before an ecclesiastical legislature do not differ between denominations. In the functioning political processes, the similarities between denominations and their various agencies are great.

New Patterns of Church Politics

Church personnel are likely to resist any acknowledgment that the actual political processes of churches change radically in the course of time. In spite of differences in formal polity, however, the denominational structures of American churches are moving toward a common pattern. In order to see this it is more instructive to study the actual process of church decision-making and action than to study the traditional patterns of polity. The actual governing and administrative processes of the churches involve such questions as efficiency in the use of resources, the recruitment of creative personnel who are tactful enough not to disrupt established patterns carelessly, and tensions between status levels. These are all comparable to problems in the Standard Oil Corporation, the Tennessee Valley Authority, and the National Infantile Paralysis Foundation. Churches striving to deal with such problems are faced with the moral embarrassment of expressing a loyalty to traditional patterns that are no longer their functioning ways of work.

One example of the emerging common pattern is the development of the role of the executive secretary. The formal political structures of many American Protestant denominations do not call for the existence of a "state secretary," a "conference superintendent," a "conference minister," or a "synodical executive." The allotments of power and authority made in the past did not forsee the need for the growth of ecclesiastical organizations at the state or regional level. Where they were developed these organizations did not always have important administrative and policy tasks, and such personnel as were necessary carried their duties along with regular pastoral appointments. With the development of an American society in which things can be done at a state level that were formerly done at a county level, and in which there is a growing tendency toward uniformity of procedures and materials in every voluntary association, a new level of administrative function is necessary. Men must be recommended for available pastoral assignments. Activities of the churches, such as youth work, need a center of program and administration and a rallying point of loyalty that is more personal than the national church. Congregational and presbyterian denominations find themselves with officers who function as bishops, not in the sense of elevated spiritual authorities, but in the sense of administrators of churches in a given area. Episcopal churches find their bishops functioning more and more as general administrators than as pastors and spiritual leaders in their dioceses.

The specialization of labor in the churches also creates new political posts and processes. Expert knowledge is required in the areas of religious education, youth work, social action, church extension, city work, rural work, and stewardship. The means by which the churches execute their mission in these spheres have become technical. The knowledge required is not available without special training or talent. Specialization of function leads to specialization of personnel. Governing boards that represent the delegated authority of bodies of the churches cannot have all the knowledge and insight necessary to come to collective decisions on technical administrative and policy matters. Increasingly boards rely upon the expert executive secretary for information, suggestions of policy, and leadership in deliberations as well as for the execution of the decisions that are made. Thus the governing boards for missions, social action, and other tasks function as "general policy" bodies, and even in this capacity they tend to become courts of approval for decisions proposed by specialists on the staff.

If specialization has changed governing boards which represent an intermediate area between staff and more inclusive deliberative bodies, the problem is even more difficult for national assemblies. Delegates gathered annually or quadrennially by the national churches do not have time in their assemblies to deliberate democratically about all the issues of policy that are necessary for the operation of an ecclesiastical institution. Agenda, and to some extent specific policies, are previously set by administrative staffs. The deliberative bodies approve in far more instances than they disapprove. Movements of revolt can be quickly detected by alert church leaders, and political processes can be put into motion to soften resistance or to avoid it altogether. The staff members and politically sensitive elite thus exercise far more power than most tables of organization and by-laws actually authorize.

The specialization of function and growth of staff exists within all the traditional polities. Church bureaucrats with similar assignments in different denominations often have more in common with one another than they have with other persons in their own denominations. These officers take cues from one another in setting the emphasis for program and church action. For a half decade, American denominations engaged in church-building capital fund campaigns; then they became interested in higher education. Presbyterian, Methodist, and Congregational denominations have a common program emphasis and in many respects common procedures as they seek funds for colleges and theological seminaries. The locus of power, whether authorized or not, has shifted to a great extent from "grassroots" and officially elected boards to the executive staff. The denominations in their functioning political and administrative structures look more and more alike.[7]

[7] Robert Michels has used the term "the iron law of oligarchy" to indicate the shift of power from the democratic base to executive personnel. The process is common to many voluntary associations. It is a function of growth in size, in geographical scope, in the complexity of factors involved in specific decisions, and in the necessity to have a concentration of social power in order to be effective in a highly bureaucratized society. See *Political Parties*, Glencoe, 1949, pp. 31 ff.

While American churches are shaped like other voluntary associations, the

In some instances staff personnel are virtually required to exercise unauthorized power in the absence of clarity about the delegation of power and authority. Paul M. Harrison has shown how some decisions by staff personnel in the American Baptist Convention, for example, must be made on the basis of calculated expediency. In the absence of authorized directives from the deliberative bodies, and of legally delegated power, a vacuum of power and authority comes into being. Decisions must be made in the light of pressing requirements without exercising the extended democratic processes that are deeply engrained in the Baptist tradition.[8] Such instances are not uncommon in church situations, just as they occur in other organizations as well. Churches are like other political communities in their need to develop many *ad hoc* patterns of life through which they can exercise their functions. The actual patterns of church political life take new forms in the light of new purposes, the social situation in which the church exists, and other interacting factors.

Troeltsch pointed out fifty years ago the need for a "sociological standpoint" from which the life of the churches could be directed. A pure fellowship of persons, or of spirit, cannot long exist without the development of definite political structures as well as doctrinal and liturgical patterns. This has been repeatedly shown in sociological studies of the processes by which a sect-type of religious movement tends to approach the highly organized Church-type. Max Weber's thesis about the necessary "routinization of charisma" suggests that the process of political growth emerges quickly after a spiritual movement comes into being. If the kernel of spirituality is to survive it must find an institutional form. Inner spiritual community cannot exist long without an organizational structure. Organizations, in turn, have their own dynamic. Once they come into being the political processes take shapes that are not always controlled immediately by the "spirit" or the theologically defined purpose; one example is the drive for institutional self-preservation in an agency after its assigned tasks have been completed. The development of political processes is a sociological necessity and not a sign of the moral degeneration of the holy com-

---

political and administrative structures of some European churches resemble state bureaucracies. In these it is still assumed (if it is not the case) that policy and administrative function are sharply distinguished, and that the latter is simply a matter of execution of policy.

[8] See Harrison, *op. cit.*, pp. 98 ff.

munity. The possibility of corruption is latent in church politics, as it is in the state or a veterans' organization or a labor union. The desire for social power as a means of ego satisfaction may be expressed by ecclesiastical officials just as it is among others. But the possible moral corruptions do not vitiate the basic requirement that churches must develop appropriate political structures. Politics is essential for the existence of Christian fellowship. The Church is a political community.

CHAPTER 4

The Church:
a Community of Language

The political order of the life of the Church is not its only institutional form. There are other persisting patterns as well. Like all human communities, the Church engages in processes of communication through the verbal symbols that are peculiarly its own. It must interpret the meaning of its language and other representations of its purposes to various generations and societies. It seeks to understand the importance of its history, and particularly the constituting events in its life. These functions must be fulfilled in order for the Church to remain an historically and socially identifiable community through time and across cultural boundaries. There are patterns of life, indeed patterns of social interaction, through which these functions are executed in the Christian community.

The Problem: the unity and continuity of the Church

In this and the following three chapters attention is turned to processes by which the Christian community maintains its social identity or consistency through history. The natural character of the community and its political processes are, of course, involved in the unity and continuity. At this point, however, the concern is to illumine the character of "inner unity" and "inner continuity" through time. How can one account for the presence of an identifiable Christian outlook, ethos, and sense of oneness among Christian people? The continuity of the Church is not merely the continuity of a political institution; there is a sense of being one people with those who have gone before, and with Christians in other cultures and nations. The Church is a community in a special sense, that is, it consists of persons with a common pattern of meanings and a common outlook on existence. There is a community of persons, of subjects. The patterns of life and thought in the Church are historically consistent enough to be identified as Christian. The question can be asked in terms more congenial to theological ways of thinking. How can the event and person of Jesus Christ be contemporaneous with each succeeding generation, and cross the linguistic and cultural boundaries? How is a common loyalty preserved and extended? The theologian is likely to answer, "By the work of the Holy Spirit." The approach to continuity and social identity of the Church in these chapters, however, is made through concepts and language developed by social philosophy.

The general framework within which the Church's social consistency takes place can be briefly sketched. The community of Christians maintains its social identity and inner unity through the internalization of meanings represented objectively in certain documents, symbols, and rites. The continuity of the Church has a double reference: on the one hand to the representations of Christ in documents and symbols, and on the other hand to the internalization of the meaning of Christ by members of the community. The meanings that become subjective, internal, and focal for persons are carried objectively, and thus potentially as meanings, in the Bible, the creeds, the symbols and rites of the Church. In one sense these objects exist independently. The Bible remains a book with readable words whether or not it is attached to a congregation, a denomination, or a believer. A creed remains a literary work available for men to read whether or not they are committed to what it says. Christian symbols, liturgies, and the written history of the Church are objects in their own right. They can exist without being interpreted, understood, or believed in. They are relatively fixed; they remain the same through history and across cultures. To be sure, translations take place and revisions are made, but these objects have a more independent status than do the beliefs, attitudes, and outlooks of the human beings that make up the continuing community. Their objective character makes them less vulner ble to flux and distortion. The existence of these things as "objects" carrying the distinctively Christian meanings makes possible the identifiable community of "subjects" who make up the Church.

` The Church is a community of subjects, of persons who share meanings and values, and who transmit these through time and across space to others. But obviously, not every gathering of persons with a common loyalty and shared meanings is the Church. Just as the Church does not exist in the objects alone (i.e., in the Bible, creeds, Christian symbols, and liturgy), so it does not exist in any random gathering of people with a common ethos. The community is identifiable as the Church because *particular* meanings inform the personal lives of members and their life together. These meanings have a common objective reference for all. The Bible, creeds, symbols, liturgy, and written history of the Church are objective representations of the common subjective life of the Church. Identity in history and across cultures depends upon the internalization of meanings carried potentially in these objects. The objects do not constitute the Church unless they inform the purposes of individuals and the ethos of a group. It is the internalization of the particular meanings carried by these objects that distinguishes the life of the Church from that of other communities of loyalty and purpose.

The concepts of Emile Durkheim can be used to restate this basic thesis. A community must have its "collective representations," i.e., the symbols, rites, and beliefs that distinguish it from other communities. These collective representations have an existence of their own; they are objective in form. But they are meaningful only insofar as they express the "collective consciousness" of the community, and in turn evoke the meanings that constitute the community's particularity. Jesus Christ can be understood as collective representation of the Christian community, indeed as its "totem symbol." Symbols of Jesus Christ evoke at least a vaguely common response from all members of the Christian community. The Church could not be distinguished from other communities unless it had its own center of meaning and some representations of this center.[1] Jesus Christ must be given specific objective symbolic form if he is to function as a representation. This form

---

[1] The conceptual framework developed by Durkheim is of limited usefulness in the interpretation of the Church. Two points of ambiguity have serious consequences: (1) Are the meanings of collective representations merely projections from the collective consciousness of the group? (2) Does collective consciousness really exist *sui generis*, or where Durkheim sometimes qualifies this, how is it independent from individual consciousnesses? On both of these questions Durkheim is subtle, and thus perhaps not precise. Exposition of his theory can be found in *Sociology and Philosophy*, London, 1953, pp. 1-34; *Elementary Forms of the Religious Life*, and elsewhere. There are many critical secondary sources as well.

he has in the Bible, ecclesiastical symbols and art, liturgy, and creeds. These objects give some precision to the content and meaning of the Christian community's center of loyalty, i.e., to Jesus Christ.

In the following chapters some of the processes will be designated through which the meanings carried in the objective representations become personal and existential. The Church is distinguishable from other communities both by its objective signs and symbols and its inner life and spirit. Meanings exist only potentially in the objects, e.g., the Bible; they become personal and actual in the community through certain processes. Four aspects of the internalization can be designated: (1) A process of *communication* exists in the Church through the language and other symbols that give social identity to this community. The Church is a community of *language*. (2) A process of *interpretation* exists through which the meanings of the Church's language and symbols become personal in different generations and cultures. The tasks of the theologian, preacher, and educator in the Church are interpretive tasks. (3) A process of *understanding and re-living* the past events in the life of the Church intensifies the identification of persons with the community. The Church is a community of memory. (4) There is a self-conscious *commitment*, or acknowledgment of belief, that designates persons as members of the community. This self-consciousness is sustained and nourished by participation in the *action* of the Church. Through these processes the Church has its social unity and identity; they make possible its continuity in time as a community of subjects or persons with a common loyalty and a common ethos.

The Church: a community of language

Members of the Church have a common language; the community has a set of significant symbols that are its own, and through which its particular meanings are communicated. The language of the Church functions socially in a way comparable to a national language or the technical language of a profession such as medicine or law. Knowledge of the special language, and facility in its use, are two of the marks of belonging to a nation or to a profession. So in the Church the outer boundaries of the historical Christian community are set by familiarity or unfamiliarity with its language. The inner core is in part designated by an intense use of the particular language of Christians. As a community of language, however, neither an inner core nor an outer boundary can be sharply drawn in the Church. The verbal symbols that give identity to the Church make up only one of the special languages that its members use. They belong to nations, families, professions, trades, and voluntary societies, each of which also has its particular verbal symbols. The Church's language is not used exclusively by any person or group, for everyone, particularly in modern society, has several points of social identification. Further, the Church's language is a public language and thus the outer boundary cannot be sharply designated. Its speech has penetrated the speech of Western Culture, and increasingly affects cultures not closely bound to the history of the Church. Finally, different churches emphasize different aspects of the Church's language. Indeed, particular churches and traditions can be identified in part by their selection of certain key words as central for the communication of the Church's meanings. The language of the Lutheran community is in some respects different from that of the Methodist and Anglican communities.

The Source of the Church's Language: the Bible

The Bible is the principle source of the Church's language. The identity of the Church is maintained by its use of the words and significant concepts of the Bible. Though other important symbols exist in the life of the Church, language remains the socially most important mode of communication.[2] The particular language of the Church is the language of the Bible. The words and meanings that give Christian identity to individuals have their source in the Bible. Without familiarity with the Bible (or literature derived from the Bible) through speech and reading, the identity of the Church would not be historically maintained. The meanings that marked the people of Israel and the primitive Church are carried in the stories, songs, discursive literature, and moral teachings of the Bible. The Bible has been the source of the Church's language through the centuries; it is the source of the Church's language in many nations and cultures. Communication through the language of the Bible sustains and develops the social

[2] A vast literature has developed on the social function of language. Cassirer, Urban, Sapir, Langer, and others have made major contributions in this area. The principal source of the framework for the present chapter, however, is the work of George Herbert Mead. In *Mind, Self, and Society*, Chicago, 1934, Mead develops a theory of social behaviorism in which language plays a major role. Through communication in a pattern of significant symbols the self takes on the meanings of the community in which it grows. Mead was a naturalist and a determinist, and the present author is not, though I find much truth in the types of explanation that Mead gives for the emergence of self and the development of community.

identity and continuity of the Christian community. The Bible has a significant social function.

Oversimplified implications from the fundamental conception of the Bible as the source of the Church's language must be avoided. Obviously, in several senses there is more than one Biblical language. Obviously also, there are many groups within the Christian community and thus disagreement on what constitutes the proper Christian language.

In several senses the Bible has more than one language. It was written in Hebrew and Greek; and there are many types of literature and many points of view represented in it. Obviously, the Biblical language of the American churches is neither Greek nor Hebrew. The Bible must be translated and retranslated in order to fulfill its social function; Greek and Hebrew texts in the modern world are socially useless except to scholars. The problems of translation illustrate the historical and social function of language in the Church. The translator seeks to retain the original meaning of the text; this preserves the historical identity of the community. He tries to overcome his bondage to his modern language and culture in order to understand the meaning of texts within the context of their first writing and speaking. If the Bible is to function as a document bearing the same meanings through history, the ideas its authors meant to convey must be understood insofar as possible. The translator, however, also seeks to give contemporary meaning to the text. Indeed his task is to make the original meaning contemporarily meaningful to the readers. Thus ideas expressed in the thought forms and vocabularies of societies in the past must be made intelligible and clear in the thought forms and vocabularies of modern societies.

The translator is a communicator; he has a social function in the Church. The words and concepts that he uses have a double social reference. They must be true to what was expressed by an earlier community, and they must communicate meaning to a contemporary community. Accuracy is required to preserve the integrity of expressions that have given historical identity to the Church. But the words used must evoke meaningful common responses from modern readers. The Church judges the adequacy of translation, then, in the light of a double reference: to the precision with which the original meanings are preserved and to the effectiveness by which they are communicated in a culturally relative situation.

Those who argue that it is necessary to know Greek and Hebrew in order properly to understand the Bible assume that the meanings are so closely bound to the style and words of original texts that they cannot be precisely understood apart from such knowledge. Those who argue for free translations in a highly contemporary idiom in turn fall into the temptation to distort the continuity of meaning. All translations, however, must perform a social function; they make the Biblical language significant as a medium of communication in a particular culture and historical period.

The manifold character of Biblical language is not exhausted by its translations and early texts. The literary styles obviously differ. Textual critics have classified the writings of the Pentateuch on the basis of characteristics of vocabulary and style. The question of whether the Letter to the Ephesians is an authentic Pauline document is answered in part on the evidence of literary similarities and differences between Ephesians and the letters of which the Pauline authorship is unquestioned. More important than difference in vocabulary and style is the difference between the basic types of writing, as each is appropriate to a special purpose or reflects a point of view. The priestly codes in the Old Testament are different in character from the poetry of the Psalms and from the expressions of moral judgment in the prophetic writings. The languages of the Bible reflect the particular purposes of its various authors. The different points of view of the narrators of the gospel accounts of the life and ministry of Jesus can be determined through analysis of characteristic words and phrases of each. Language is a bearer of meaning, and diversity in language points to diversity in meaning. No simple pattern of unity of the Biblical language can be extracted from or imposed upon the texts.

The diversity of the Bible is reflected in the special emphases of various groups and movements within the Christian community. The Lutheran tradition, for example, favors the writings of St. Paul; the Anglican tradition favors the Johannine literature. Neither tradition uses exclusively one or the other section of the Bible, but there are apparent affinities for certain authors. The legal codes of the Old Testament and the moral teachings of Jesus are interpreted by some groups in a legalistic way, by others more freely. The writings of Amos and the other prophets seem to be more meaningful in a period of social unrest and crisis than in a time of peace and prosperity. Calvin's appreciation of the Old Testament as a guide for the Christian life was greater than Luther's. One generation of Christians finds the Pauline literature to be more meaningful and profound than another; another generation focuses on the gospel stories of Jesus. The diversity of Biblical language lends itself to diversity of emphases and use by particular churches and movements, with their own historical traditions and historical situations.

In spite of the churches' selectivity in emphases, the Bible provides a language for the whole Church. The traditional prayers and forms of piety are imbued with Biblical language and meaning. Phrases and concepts that have a special significance for a particular group are used nevertheless by all, e.g., justification by faith. The reading of lectionaries in many churches makes the congregations familiar with various portions from the whole Bible. Private reading and study of the entire Bible continues.

The presence of the Bible as the principal source of the Church's language makes possible a common ethos in the community. The meanings of the Church are informed by the Bible; the Bible bears objectively the Church's language. The language is used as a means of communication by Christian groups in particular times and places, and thus exists in relation to changing communities and circumstances. The fact of this relationship to specific communities, however, does not imply that the meaning of the Bible is simply projected from the churches. Rather there is a common objective point of reference over which controversy can rage and from which selections can be made. This common language sustains the Church, for it is the language of all Christians.

For example, the phrase "justification by faith" has a special historical significance for Protestants, since both Luther and Calvin placed it at the center of their reforming work. Yet it is common to the whole Church. Traditional and perennial theological discussions take place over its precise meaning. It has been the center of arguments between Protestants and Catholics; it is closely related to the basic issues between Augustinians and Pelagians. In Protestantism the phrase is involved in the interpretation of the nature of the Christian life; whether justification implies moral sanctification in this life, or only an alteration of man's relation to God. The specification of its meaning by particular groups does not exclude its importance to the whole Church. The whole Church acknowledges the significance of the Pauline epistles within the phrase is stressed. The initiative of God in saving men is acknowledged by most of the Church. In spite of its historically Protestant identification, the phrase and its meaning belong to all of Christendom. It is part of the language that gives identity to the

Christian community, and differentiates it from other religious and secular communities. The Bible provides the common language of the Church.

Communication and the Christian Community

Communication makes possible the development of an identifiable Christian group. The Bible provides the language through which communication takes place in the Church. Persons are identified with the Church as they convey meanings to one another in the language of Christians. Meanings carried in language become a part of the mind and selfhood of persons as they speak and hear. The language of the Bible, as the language of communication in the Church, makes possible the existence of a common life among Christians.

Language is obviously related to community through the speech of persons. Several questions must be raised in order to understand the implications of this truism. What is the relation of Christian language and Christian community to the selfhood of individual Christians? How does a community's language affect its members? How do members affect one another through language? A social theory of the self, such as that developed by G. H. Mead, gives some insight into this process.

The Church is one of the communities that form the personal character of Christians. The Church's language is one of several that a person learns. In learning the Church's language and using it as a means of communication he becomes identified with the Christian community. A person comes into being through participation in the life of various communities. The social groups are the "generalized others" whose characteristics one absorbs. Family, social class, peer group, and Church all function as socializing agents in the development of a person. What each of these communities stands for is embodied in part in its characteristic language. The meanings and values of each group are given symbolic and objective expression in its speech. Through the use of the speech that embodies the values of a particular community, persons take into themselves its attitudes and outlook. The national character of Americans or Frenchmen is an expression of an ethos carried in part by the symbols that belong in a peculiar way to each nation.

The Church is one of the "generalized others" or "reference groups" to which Christians belong. Although it is difficult precisely to designate and locate, there is a pattern of meaning and life that characterizes the Church, and which in turn is reflected in the outlook of its members. The language of the Bible, the liturgy, the hymns, and the testimonies of personal religious experience all impress meanings in persons. The patterns of a person's life and thought are conditioned by the symbols of communication in the Church. Christians cannot understand themselves without noting the importance of the meanings carried in the Church's language, or their participation in the Christian community.

Participation in the life of the Church is obviously not the only determining factor in the character of an individual. The language of advertisers, novelists, friends, and others all have their impact. Further, social determination is not the only factor involved in the development of selfhood. There are also inner drives and powers, and the capacity to act. A person can choose to relate himself to ideas or groups through his self-determination. With these and other necessary qualifications, however, it can still be said that the language of the Church conditions the meanings and values of its members. The ethos of the Church, transmitted through language, is impressed into conscience and outlook and thus affects action. The use of its particular language gives the Christian community as a whole its social identity. Its members share meanings in common as they share a language.

The Church must continue to use its own language if it desires to transmit its meanings and values from person to person and generation to generation. If it equates the meanings of its language too easily with that of another community it risks the loss of its identity. For example, if religious terms are given equivalents in the language of psychoanalysis without qualification, the two communities are identified with each other and the loss of the individuality and uniqueness of each is risked. Yet some process of translation or interpretation must be undertaken in order to make contact with communities and languages that exist alongside the Church. Religious language becomes esoteric and "sacred," and finally socially meaningless, if it does not find a point of relation to other meanings and language. The Church's social identity depends, then, upon a twofold process: the continued use of the Biblical language within the common life of the Church, and its use in interpreting and understanding general human experience as it exists outside the Church. Decline in the use of its language leads to a weakening of the marks of differentiation between the Church and other communities. Use of the language as a means of communication in the

Church strengthens a sense of common purpose and outlook among Christians.[3]

The Church's social continuity and identity is dependent upon the use of the Bible as the source of its language. The modern Christian community has continuity with the ancient Church in part because both have the same set of significant symbols. The process of communication in the Church has been unbroken through its history. In the definition of the canon the early Church set limits to the language that is appropriate for its life. The Bible it shaped has provided the language that is read, preached, sung, prayed, studied, and discussed in the churches. Various bases of selectivity and emphasis have existed, but the whole Bible has been available throughout the Church's history. Reformation in the community has taken place as men have returned to the Biblical language, and sought to throw off language that is uncongenial to the Church's purpose and nature. Yet no reformation has brought an absolute discontinuity in the history of the community. Reformers find certain texts and meanings to be uniquely true to the essence of the Church's life. Movements that refuse to use the language of the Bible, or that add another language to it, become socially marginal to the whole Church, e.g., modern Unitarianism, Mormonism, and Christian Science. The existence of the Bible as an objective linguistic expression of the meanings of the Church, and the continuous communication within the Church through this language, have made possible the social continuity and unity of the Christian community.

Special Languages and Special Christian Groups

Separate groups within the Church exist through the continued use of the language that bears their special interpretations of Christianity. Out of reformations intended to bring the whole Church to new life have come movements characterized in part by particular languages and meanings. Creeds have been written in order to distill the essence of what the Bible means, and these in turn have given historical particularity to separate movements within the Church. The ecumenical

[3] Mead's understanding of the self lies in the background of this exposition. See his *Mind, Self, and Society*, especially pp. 144-78, but throughout, and the essay "The Genesis of the Self and Social Control" in *The Philosophy of the Present*, Chicago, 1932, pp. 176-95. The persisting structure of selfhood that comes into being through communication and other forms of social interaction Mead calls the "me." The possibility of novel action lies in the "I" aspect of the self. Mead believed that if we had adequate knowledge "novel" actions could be predicted; he was a thoroughgoing determinist, or social behaviorist.

creeds express what the whole Church once agreed on as the summary of truth. Yet even they were a basis of social differentiation; Nestorians, Copts, and other groups came into being through the exclusion that resulted from the process of creed formation. The Augsburg Confession and the Formula of Concord, the Westminster Confession and other creeds are examples of churches' efforts to be precise about what the Bible does and does not say. Acceptance or rejection of a particular creed gives social shape to particular societies of Christians, for the creed becomes the test for membership. Through the language and use of creeds, particular churches differentiate themselves from one another. The creed-forming process continues to have a social function; a confession of faith continues to be a linguistic device that defines the boundaries of particular Christian movements. A recent example is the World Council of Churches' confession of "Jesus Christ as God and Savior." An alteration of this formula would change the social character of the Council. The present language excludes the membership of such groups as American Unitarians and Universalists. A language acceptable to them would probably exclude the Eastern Orthodox and other churches.

Creeds are not the only form in which religious language is particularized. Characteristic ways of preaching, the use of certain hymns, the liturgy and other aspects of communication in the churches define their social boundaries. For example, Southern Baptist Churches in the United States have a distinctive ethos and social identity without the benefit of an authoritative creed. It is expressed and sustained in the style and language of sermons, prayers, hymns, and promotion materials. The introduction of different patterns of language, e.g., the use of non-Southern Baptist Sunday School material, creates tension in the denomination, for the meanings that have established its identity are thereby brought into question. In churches with established liturgical traditions the language of the liturgy functions to maintain consistency and social identity. The Book of Common Prayer, for example, provides a basis upon which the Church of England and its daughter churches nourish their distinctive qualities of common life. A radical change in the liturgy would disrupt the unity of the existing community. Pietism has a characteristic language, stressing self-examination and personal sins, Bible reading and free prayer, and identification with the sufferings and death of Christ. Christian pietists from various denominations feel a kinship in spirit and attitude through these media.

Certain patterns of language fall into disuse in the Church or in par-

ticular Christian movements. Change of language often indicates a
change in the character of the community. For example, the social gospel movement of four decades ago expressed itself in terms of "building
the Kingdom of God," or "doing what Jesus would do." The social mission of the Church is rarely expressed in these terms at the present
time. The change represents a new development both in the theological foundations and the practical tactics of the movement. Two generations of Christians equally committed to the social mission of the
Church can be distinguished by the language through which they understand themselves and state their purposes.

A particular movement in the Church must consistently use its
particular language if it is to persist through the generations. If a modern Lutheran Church would stop teaching and preaching in historically
Lutheran concepts, its bond to the Lutheran tradition would obviously
weaken. When Methodism uses language more congenial to contemporary religious life than that of John Wesley, its character as a religious
group changes. One outcome is a spawning of new groups who seek
to retain the genuinely Wesleyan language and meanings. In various
religious movements there are periodic efforts to return to the language of the founder or to the creative historical period of the group.
Lutherans would purge their tradition of the increments of orthodoxy,
pietism, and liberalism by a return to the evangelical language and
theology of Martin Luther. Some Methodists would return to Wesley.
Efforts of restoration assume that the most distinctive religious language comes into being during the period when a reform movement is
differentiating itself most intensively from the corruption or lifelessness
of old forms. Restoration of the images used by the founder will presumably in turn restore the uniqueness of the denomination or movement.

When the importance of particular languages diminishes, the occasion for new social groupings in the Church occurs. Loyalty to particular languages diminishes in two ways. On the one hand, in a
process of secularization or a period of latitudinarianism distinctive
meanings appear to be unimportant. Thus indifference to religious
language becomes the basis for new combinations of religious groups.
On the other hand, the recovery of the Biblical language as the common ground underlying existing differences enables new social forms
to occur. In American Protestantism the lack of interest in the particularities of religious doctrines, and the general enthusiasm for re-
building the moral and social world (an enthusiasm the churches

shared with other reform movements), fostered the growth of Protestant co-operation in the early decades of this century. Urban councils of churches could divide cities on the basis of comity agreements in part on the assumption that the distinctiveness of Methodism or Congregationalism was really unimportant. The Federal Council of Churches could bring traditions into co-operative activity by giving attention to the practical tasks of the Church and ignoring potentially divisive theological statements. Disuse of distinctive religious language becomes the occasion for new social forms.

On the other hand, churches rediscover a Biblical language that is more important than the specifications of denominational creeds or hymns. What has been called "the rediscovery of the Bible" in Protestant circles gives new enthusiasm to movements to unite churches and find new forms of common work. The current emphasis on the "Biblical foundations" of every particular work of the Church from preaching to stewardship and social action is in part motivated by a desire to foster ecumenicity in one social form or another. If the Biblical basis for social action, Christian education, evangelism, and pastoral counseling can be established, presumably the barriers of denominationalism will begin to crumble. The renewed acceptance of the Bible as normative for the life and thought of the Church makes possible new forms of Christian community.

The Church is a language community. Its identity across space and time has been sustained through its continuous communication in the significant symbols derived from a common source, the Bible. Denominations and other movements within the Church are communities whose continued identity depends in part on the use of their particular emphases in the Biblical language and thought, or their own statements of faith and purpose. The existence of the Church is threatened when new languages are substituted for the Christian language. The sense of unity in the Church is intensified when the distinctively Christian language is maintained in the churches and provides men with the framework within which they understand themselves, the world, and God.

Communication is a process of social interaction. It is a natural process; it exists in all human communities. The identity of a nation is a function of its ethos as it is expressed in language. It may be the language of "blood and soil," or it may be the language of democracy. The identity of the business community or the community of physicians is sustained by the use of the language of each. The process of communication is common to all forms of human community. Neither the existence of a language nor the process of communication is unique to the Church. The *particular* language that the Church uses, bearing the meanings that are distinctive to its life, marks its differentiation from other communities. Through the use of its language, drawn from the primary source, the Bible, the Church impresses its meanings on persons, and develops a common life.

Communication, however, involves interpretation. The Church is not a community in which the same words are incanted over and over. Meaning is not necessarily internalized through familiarity with words. To be significant, symbols must be interpreted themselves and used to interpret the world in which men live. Thus the Church is also a community of interpretation.

CHAPTER 5

The Church:
a Community of Interpretation

The process of interpretation pervades the life of the Christian community. The Bible, Christian symbols, and liturgy are interpreted to each generation, to various cultural groups, and to individual persons. The Church is interpreted by teachers and preachers in order that its members may understand it. The world is interpreted in the light of the meanings that bind Christians together. The personal existence of man is interpreted through the doctrines of the Church. The Church influences the world by the interpretation of its message. Different persons have different interpretive tasks in the Church. Theologians interpret the Bible in the light of philosophy, ethics, artistic symbols, and various canons of scholarship. Historians interpret the Church's past. Preachers interpret the Church's beliefs to their congregations. Educators interpret in a way that is appropriate to particular levels of intellectual maturity. Interpretation is an important aspect of social interaction.

Interpretation: a three-point process

The process of interpretation always involves three points of reference: what is interpreted, an interpreter, and the persons to whom he interprets. The process of interpretation makes words and images meaningful to persons. That which exists objectively is related to man's experience and ability to understand. Many different matters are the object of interpretation in the Church—a person such as Amos or Jesus Christ, a pattern of church life such as its liturgy, ideas such as the doctrine of atonement, a state of human affairs in the world such as war, a book such as the Bible, a personal crisis such as death. The purposes of interpretation differ. It may be to win a convert to the Church, to enlighten one who is already a member, to make a moral judgment, to offer consolation, to clarify the Church's purpose, to transmit the heritage of the community, or to influence political or other decisions. The persons to whom interpretation is made differ according to the purpose. It may be directed to those within the congregation or assembly; it may be directed to those outside. It may be directed to men of power in secular society, or to an individual involved in a crisis. There are various interpretive functions in the Church, e.g., preaching, teaching, counseling, and writing.

The interpreter needs adequate knowledge of both the object (e.g., the meaning of Easter), and the persons to whom he is interpreting (e.g., a class of ten-year-old children). Preachers must know the Bible and basic convictions of the Church, and they must know the situations from which their congregations listen. The pastor must know the dynamics of human personality in order to understand the man he counsels; he must know the religious resources of healing if he is to function as a Christian pastor. The prophet needs to understand both the conditions upon which he pronounces moral judgment and the principles in the light of which he speaks.

Interpretation is a process of relating ideas and persons to each other. The interpreter brings principles and commitments to his task. He interprets the Bible in the light of what he thinks is a proper estimate of the human situation; or he interprets the human situation in the light of what he thinks are proper principles of Biblical exposition. Much of the interpretation in the Church relates *meanings* to *persons*. The meanings of the Church continue because they are personally and socially significant for its members; that is, because they are effectively interpreted. Interpretation is a community-sustaining process.[1] Various functions and forms of the process can be seen if we look at the tasks of some important interpreters in the Church: theologians, preachers, teachers, and prophets. The function of each of these groups in the community is important for the others.

Theologians as interpreters

The division of labor in the Church assigns various functions to various offices. The effective action of men through these offices sustains and extends the Christian community. One such vocation is that of the theologian. He is the specialist in the knowledge of God, the ultimate object of loyalty in the community. Since the task of interpreting the nature of God involves reference to the Bible, philosophy, the moral situation of man, history, and the institutional life of the Church, the general theological program of the Church has a division of labor within it. The theological curriculum of universities and seminaries is designed to facilitate the task of interpreting the nature of God in relation to various theoretical and practical problems. The meaning of God must be clarified in relation to specific problems and needs, e.g., a particular philosophical attack such as Nietzsche's, or a particular practical issue such as the race problem.

Since the distinctive language that the Christian community uses in its knowledge of God is found in the Bible, the theological function of the Church is carried out with primary reference to the Scriptures. They are the receptacle for the Church's traditional meaning and interpretation of God. Indeed, the Bible is itself an interpretation of the meaning of God in relation to Jesus Christ, to the human experiences of sin and guilt, and to the historical events in the life of the people of Israel. The social unity and continuity of the Church requires that the Bible hold the primary position in the theological work of the Church. It is the interpretation of the Biblical understanding of God that makes the Church a distinctive religious community.

The theologian, however, stands between the Bible and some other point. He may determine his work to be the proper interpretation of the Bible for the Church; thus he keeps in mind the situation of the

[1] The philosophy of Josiah Royce is the basis upon which the framework of the present chapter is built, as the philosophy of Mead was for the preceding chapter. See his *The Problem of Christianity*, Vol. II, pp. 207 ff., p. 150 ff., *et passim*. John E. Smith's *Royce's Social Infinite*, New York, 1950, pp. 69 ff., contains an excellent discussion of the theory of interpretation in Royce's thought.

Church as he engages in his interpretations. Or a particular philosophy, such as existentialism or idealism, may be the other pole of his activity. The way in which the theologian works depends upon those to whom he seeks to make clear the nature of God. Interpretation is conversation; conversation in theology is between the theologian, as he is identified with the Church and the Bible, and the persons who have raised the questions he feels compelled to answer. Much dialogue consequently is between theologians; it is the interpretation of God in the light of points of view that a theologian believes to be distorted or inadequate. The dialogue may be between the theologian and the artists and writers who express the spirit of the times; or between the theologian and those who represent a crisis in the Church or State.

Within the community of professional theologians there are inter-dependent functions. The Biblical scholars have a proper role, as do the ethicists and the practical theologians. The Biblical scholars clarify the meaning of the Bible in relation to historical evidence, literary styles, linguistic problems, and what they take to be the most significant themes in the book. Historians interpret the various expressions of the Church's understanding of God in its creeds, liturgies, and organizational forms. They interpret the Church's relations to political, social, and intellectual movements with which it has been engaged. They clarify the impact of the Church and its work on other groups and institutions, and the conditioning effects of other movements on the Church. Systematic theologians bring the Church's beliefs into a coherent pattern around a center of meaning that is to them significant. The whole may be interpreted in the light of a definite understanding of the meaning of Jesus Christ, e.g., as a moral ideal; or it may be in the light of a dominant motif such as *agape;* or a philosophical commitment such as linguistic analysis; or a particular understanding of the human situation, e.g., man's ontological anxiety. Ethicists interpret the moral problems and condition of man in the light of the Church's knowledge of God in order to give some direction to Christian behavior. The practical theologians interpret the various functions of ministers and the congregations in the light of the purpose of the Church. They are concerned to clarify the implications of the Church's message for man's anxiety and grief, for his place of work and life in human society, and for various levels of intellectual and personal maturity.

Theologians become occupied with the interpretation of specific issues from time to time. During the totalitarian crisis of the 1930's much theology pertained to the proper status of the nation and the state in the light of the Bible and its implications. Currently much attention is given to a proper understanding of the Church itself. The study program of the Department of Faith and Order in the World Council of Churches illustrates this concern. The unity and disunity of the Church are placed under the scrutiny of men who seek to understand the meaning of Jesus Christ, of worship and liturgy, of tradition, and of institutional factors for the life of the community. The program assumes that the Church cannot be properly interpreted theologically without a consideration of both its center of loyalty and belief and its involvement in historical patterns and social structures.

The process of theological interpretation continues through history because the object of the Church's trust, God, must be seen in ever new relationships. The specific implications of the Church's belief differ in the United States, Denmark, the Soviet Union, and the Republic of Indonesia. The Church's relation to the romanticism of the nineteenth century was different from the struggles of the sixteenth century, and from the requirements of the present age. Particular systems are shaped in the light of other systems or intellectual tendencies; Reinhold Niebuhr shapes his thought in relation to the liberal assumptions of American Protestantism and American culture; Karl Barth defines himself against Scheiermacher, orthodox Lutherans, and various other persons and groups. The changing historical context in which the Church finds itself, with new patterns of thinking, new historical documents, new moral problems, and new creative theologians, makes the theological process a never-ending one. The community strives for clarity about itself and its object of loyalty in the light of new situations. It must reshape the specific definitions of its purpose in the light of a changing milieu. New relationships demand new awareness of the Church's distinctive beliefs and patterns of life. Theological interpretation is an essential function in retaining the character of the Christian community.

The Church constantly questions the adequacy of particular interpretations of its life and beliefs. In the process of relating knowledge of God to particular situations some of the distinctive elements of the Church may be hidden or lost. For example, in speaking to cultural despair, the message of the Church may be so infused with an existentialist pattern of thought that no distinction between them remains. Parties form around various interpretations; parties are social groups, and may issue in new social institutions. The division of the Reformation churches among Lutheran, Calvinist, and Anabaptist theologies is evidence of the power of theological interpretations to form new communities. The Church looks for criteria by which the merits of various points of view can be judged. For example, in the relating of the message of the Church to a concrete culture, how is the essence of the Church's knowledge of God preserved? Or, how does a denomination decide what other churches are "true" enough to share its communion service? Churches have found ways to deal with such problems.

The terms used to designate the relative degrees of adequacy have traditionally been *orthodoxy, heterodoxy,* and *heresy.* These indicate relative distance from an authoritative standard of correctness. Where politically authorized persons have made judgments of heresy and decreed that groups who hold such opinions are outside the Church, a process of social differentiation has taken place. Churches have maintained consistency through the use of creeds as the test of orthodoxy and through the ecclesiastical courts as the seat of political power. A sharp line between adequate and inadequate theology is hard to draw, however, in the light of the interpretive character of theological thinking. Some denominations accept this, at least implicitly, in their refusal to make a particular interpretation the standard test for membership in a congregation, or for ordination to the ministry. The refusal to determine such a standard may become the occasion for a great latitude of theological opinion within a group. The variety may be defended on the ground of freedom of conscience, or on the assumption that absence of legal norms makes for creativity and effectiveness in Church life and thought. The social effect of such tolerance, however, is often a denomination without consensus, not only about dogma, but also about purposes and ways of work. A state of *anomie* (normlessness) with reference to proper belief can lead to confusion in common life, or to the use of expediency as the proper standard for action. The Church faces the possible consequences of latitudinarianism, or "modernism."

"Modernism" is a form of heterodoxy. It has taken place on many occasions in the history of the Church. Churches have sought to interpret their truths in the language and thought forms of various ages. To do so has been a pedagogical advantage, or it has been useful in explaining the faith of the Church to various generations of cultured despisers. Often the motivation has been "relevance," i.e., seeking an interpretation that is pertinent to a specific but transitory situation. Implicit in the desire to relate the Church to secular societies and thought forms is the danger of weakening loyalty and commitment to traditional theological norms. The Bible as the source of the community's understanding of God may be eclipsed by other languages, thought forms, or objects of loyalty. Interpreters may assume there is a current secular equivalent for every Christian notion, e.g., repentance is catharsis, justification by faith is absence of guilt and anxiety, and the Kingdom of God is a democratic socialist order. The strain toward heterodoxy is present wherever the Church seeks to establish a positive relation to other social and cultural movements. The boundaries of the Christian community become inclusive; they are extended to include all for whom the Bible and Christian theology have any importance as a basis for interpreting human existence. The audience may be enlarged at the price of weakening an inner consistency and the marks of identity that have distinguished the Church from other groups. Heterodoxy is a social temptation in every culture in which the Church exists, Hindu, Hellenistic, or modern Western.

Orthodoxy also has social consequences. Insistence upon precise limits within which the process of theological interpretation can take place may preserve a common core of traditional meanings and values. The distinctive elements of Christian belief may be safeguarded for the persons who accept an authorized definition of them. It may, however, restrict the scope of conversation so that the speaking and writing of the Church is intelligible only to those who are already initiated members. The theological enterprise may become esoteric; it may be meaningful only to those who know its limited vocabulary and concepts. Orthodoxy, however, does not avoid the interpretive function. Creeds cast in the language of another age must be made meaningful in the present. Theologians demonstrate astounding intellectual ingenuity in making ancient statements acceptable to persons sharing a modern world view. The orthodox churches tend to restrict the questions that a person can ask without jeopardizing his status in the community. They often lose touch with modern critical patterns of thought, though some of them demonstrate remarkable ability to use modern techniques in making their witness attractive. Orthodoxy wills to preserve certainty about the bases for Church action and life, and thus to ensure an inner discipline of the community, regardless of the cost. Orthodoxy, like modernism, is a social option for the Church.

A functioning definition of heresy or its equivalent is necessary if the Church is to determine what theological interpretations are unacceptable. A denomination or congregation cannot long express openness to every type of belief, whether related to the Biblical sources or not, and maintain its identity as a Christian community. Social chaos is the consequence of the lack of any definition of the outer limits beyond which an interpretation is invalid. If the Church as a whole cannot agree on the principles for such a determination, particular denominations and congregations can, and in effect do. The Church's survival as a distinctive community depends upon theological interpretations and judgments.

Ministers as Interpreters

In a restricted sense, the function of theological interpretation is carried out by specialists who have been trained to engage in this work. Churches and universities provide them suitable conditions in which to exercise their vocation. The professor is not, however, the only theological interpreter. The activities of the parish clergyman, insofar as they are directed and governed by the Church's knowledge of God, are expressions of his theological reflection. The point of his identification as a Christian minister is his loyalty to the Church's understanding of God, and of man in relation to God. The minister stands between the Church's understanding of God and the needs of a particular congregation or parish as he sees them in the light of his belief. His position is second to none in importance in relating persons to Christian meanings, and meanings to persons, and thus in sustaining and expanding the Christian community. Each of his specific functions, such as preaching and counseling, involves a process of interpretation.

The minister, like the theologian, needs to know the sources of the Church's particular understanding of God. He functions within the general purpose of relating men in various historical conditions to God; therefore he must know theology. The minister works within a particular organizational framework through which the imperatives of the Church's beliefs affect human society; therefore he must know the structure and functions of his institution, whether it be a congregation or a college or a denominational staff. The minister functions within a pattern of personal relationships, and exercises influence upon persons; therefore he has to understand the nature of personal interaction and the structure of human personality. The minister works within a social structure and culture which influence his institution and the persons with whom he works, whether it be an American suburb, or a West European industrial city, or a village in South India; therefore he has to understand his culture and social structure if he is to be an effective interpreter. At least these points of reference are always involved in his interpretation of his task and in his action. If he does not have knowledge of doctrine, institutions, persons, and society that an expert in each of these areas would deem to be adequate, he nevertheless functions with certain assumptions about the nature of them. The congregation or denomination that he leads is affected by his interpretation.

In his preaching the clergyman is an interpreter. He is the interpreter of the convictions of the Church to a specific group of people. His task requires a good understanding of the persons in his congregation and the values and general cultural ethos they represent. Interpretation is an important aspect of the preacher's task; he uses words in an effort to evoke a particular response from a certain group of people. The preacher's work is always theological, but the function of his office differs in two ways from the theologian's. He is not required to have a specific knowledge of the finer distinctions in the history of Christian thought, but he is required to have more precise knowledge of the special group to which he is interpreting. Preaching does not exist primarily for the sake of intellectual refinement of the minister, or for disputation of points of dogma. It is certainly not exposition for its own sake. Rather the society in which preaching takes place is concrete; it is a particular congregation of farmers and merchants, of suburban housewives and their harried husbands, of nature worshipers, or the socially disinherited. The preacher's function is to bring a particular people into a more significant relation to the meanings of the Church. Thus his interpretation keeps in view specific problems, e.g., unbelief among church members, racial crises in the community, personal crises in families. He views a concrete human community in the light of the truths to which the total Christian community adheres.

In his various other functions the persons to whom the minister interprets the Church's meanings represent even more specific purposes and problems. As pastor he make the Church significant through his counsel to an individual in his difficulties. He brings the anxieties of an alcoholic, the tensions of a marriage, the delinquency of a boy, the grief of a family, and the aspirations of a student under the light of the Church's distinctive ethos as it is expressed in the Bible and in the life of the community. The community penetrates the most intimate occasions of life through its representation by the pastor. The meanings carried in the objective expressions become significant in the moments in which men are most impressionable. The community is extended both in the intensity of the identification of persons with it, and in scope, as pastors function interpretively.

Committees, or boards of laymen in a congregation or a denomination, have designated tasks to fulfill with the assistance of ministers. Meetings of such groups are occasions in which the purposes of the Church, as they are theologically determined, become focused on very specific needs, such as securing teachers for the church school, raising money needed for the congregation and its missions, planning a new social service institution, or remodeling a sanctuary. Ministers, as representatives of the purposes of the Church, interpret the requirements of a specific function in the light of normative concerns, and thus intensify the identification of men with the community of Christians.

In American society the minister is often called upon to represent religion at civic and political celebrations. The acknowledgment of "spiritual values" and the Deity has become a part of the ritual of public life. Such occasions may provide opportunities to bring the purposes of the civic community under the influence of the Church and its beliefs. A Roman Catholic bishop, for example, interpreted the industry council proposals of the papal social encyclicals to a labor convention in the course of an invocation! In more subtle ways, the Church's influence on the secular society is exercised by the representation of the Church in civic affairs.

The Church must have effective interpreters at the level of the parish and congregation if it is to survive as a community and extend its influence and scope. The minister's interpretive skill, or lack of it, is manifest in his adaptation to rapidly changing conditions in the city or village, and especially among the persons with whom he works. He represents the Church, the meanings and values of which are not coextensive with those of his church members and culture. In his interpretations, he may identify himself with the culture and persons in such a way as to lose the distinctive objectivity of the Church's standpoint. Or he may adhere closely to a particular definition of the Church's truth at the cost of the required flexibility in changing conditions. His effectiveness in relating the message and purpose of the Church to concrete situations affects both the quality and extent of the Christian community's distinctive existence. He has an important interpretive function in maintaining both the identity and the unity of outlook of the Church.

Teachers as Interpreters

Ministers and other members of the Church engage in the necessary function of teaching. The meanings and values of the Christian community must be transmitted in each generation to persons who are becoming affiliated with it.

Teaching is sometimes understood in a highly objective way; e.g., the data of the Church's history or of the Bible are taught and learned for their own sake. Bible verses and the list of the kings of Israel can be memorized; the important dates in the history of the community can be stressed. The task of interpretation in this understanding of teaching is left to the learner, whether it be a small child, a potential convert, or a university student.

The task of the teacher is, however, often understood in a different way. The communication of ideas and information is related to the ability and readiness of the learner to comprehend them. The students vary in intellectual maturity; they bring their own predispositions to doubt or believe to the class; they have their own filtering devices through which ideas and information come. The teacher's function is to interpret ideas and information in such a way that they are taken seriously by the learners, and evoke a response that is personal in character. The learner is not the only interpreter; the teacher is also interpreter.

The Church teaches in order to convince persons. It seeks to interpret its distinctive convictions in such a way that persons are convinced of their truth. Such a function is a social necessity. The points of reference for the teacher are the objective sources of the Church's beliefs about God and man on the one hand, and the situation of the learner on the other. Not all of the complex and profound beliefs of the community can be internalized by an eight-year-old child. The interpretation of the Church's convictions to college students interested in logical rationality will be different from its interpretation to pious members eager to learn more and to believe with greater earnestness. The teacher must know the learners as well as the information and ideas to be transmitted. The instruction of the Church to Hindus or Moslems takes into account their present religious loyalties; the instruction to American middle-class children takes into account their view of the world as it is conditioned by the prosperity of an "affluent society."

Discussions among both professional religious educators and missionaries in recent decades illustrate the social functions of teaching. In the United States, the churches until recently shared with the public schools an interest in "child centered" learning. Curriculum materials and teachers focused on the growth of a wholesome "Christian" personality in children. The purpose of the Church was equated with the transmission of psychological and moral wisdom. This concern for those to whom interpretation is made led to a startling degree of ignorance of the Bible and Christian doctrine in several generations of Protestants. There was little or no identification of persons with those elements of the Church's teaching that distinguish it from other morally concerned, humanistic, and democratic communities. The distinctive character of the Church was losing its importance, and the identity of the Church was threatened. As Protestantism over the world renewed its interest in the differentiating elements in the Church's life, the programs of American religious educators were brought into a sharp debate. Revisions in curriculum stressed the transmission of the convictions and teachings of the Bible. The interpreting teachers paid more attention to that which gives the Church its identity as a special community. Faced with different age and intelligence levels, however, the problem of effective interpretation to their students continues.

The mission of the Church to non-Christians tended to be equated with the provision of social welfare and educational services motivated by love. The doctrines of the Church and the Bible were subordinated to merciful deeds. With this subordination came efforts to find a common ground of morality, or of loyalty to a Deity about whom Christians and non-Christians could agree. The preoccupation with the points of affinity led to a weakening of the specific identity of the Christian Church. The beliefs that differentiated it from other religious communities were assumed to be of little importance. All this was brought into sharp debate by theologically astute missionaries, such as Hendrik Kraemer. The debate of ideas became a policy debate within particular churches and their mission agencies. Christian groups who are minorities in their cultures need a certainty of what gives them their Christian distinctiveness if they are to survive both social hostility and the normal processes of social assimilation. Churches continue to seek patterns of interpretation that preserve the content of the Church's message while establishing contact with non-Christian religious groups and cultures. The survival and growth of the younger churches depend upon their effectiveness.

Evangelists as Interpreters

Pastors, missionaries, and teachers function as evangelists, as do those for whom this is a special task in the Church's division of labor. Evangelism is the interpretive process through which the Church brings persons from outside the community into its life, and those at the periphery into the center. It is an effort through preaching and other activity to evoke a sense of need in persons for the meanings and values that the Church represents. It seeks to relate men self-consciously to God as the Christian community knows him. This is done by interpreting the situation of man in such a way that he is convinced of the validity of the answer given by the evangelist. Effective evangelists are skillful interpreters.

In order to evoke the desired religious response, the evangelist first gives a religious interpretation of the plight of man. Potential converts have to be convinced that the religious interpretation of their condition is valid before they accept answers in religious terms. Men may be egocentric, domineering, and hungry for power. This state can be interpreted in psychological terms, or as the result of social conditioning, or as a manifestation of sin. If the Church is to provide the salvation, the needy person must be persuaded that sin or evil is the root of the problem. Guilt and anxiety can be interpreted as the result of lack of parental affection, of harassed life in modern urban society, or of man's alienation and estrangement from God and his disobedience to God. International tensions can be interpreted to stem from political factors, economic factors, racial factors, or from the ignorance and rebelliousness of God's children. If the evangelist persuasively interprets the situations so that the religious factor is believed to be dominant, he is likely to evoke the response that he desires.

The skills of the mass public evangelist common in the United States are even more defined, for the evangelist knows how to interpret the "mood" or the emotions of his audience. Under the stimulation of certain conditions (e.g., folk music and folk stories) an audience "warms up." It becomes predisposed to respond enthusiastically to both the analysis and the answer of the evangelist.

Whether the evangelist be a theologian-preacher making sophisticated students aware of their need "to accept their acceptance," or the jazzy showman of well-organized revivals, the effectiveness of his interpretation both of man's condition and the Church's answer is the key to the growth of the Christian community through evangelism. Churches seek new patterns for this function; for example, the illuminating significance of modern drama and poetry are turned on the plight of man. The evocative power of contemporary concepts of "meaninglessness," "despair," "estrangement," and other images is used. Language is borrowed from various sources to interpret the needs of men for which the Church provides a satisfaction. Different patterns of interpretation are fitted to the various audiences—to adolescents, to "beat generation" urban sophisticates, to gentlemen of ivy league *savoir-faire*, to Negroes in urban tenements or rural slums, to migrants moving from rural America to its industrial cities. Evangelistic patterns of interpretation are necessary to sustain and enlarge the Church.

Prophets as Interpreters

The Church, like the people of Israel before it, has had its prophets, whose function it is to call the community from its preoccupation with various idols back to its true form and purpose. The critical, prophetic function is essential for the preservation of the particular loyalty that the Church proclaims. Not only do the prophets interpret the Church; they are the Church's interpreters of the historical forces that shape human destiny. Though there is no formal office of prophet, men function in this way in the Church. They are the religious-moral judges of the Christian community and its relations to other communities.

The prophet has a singular sense of rightness, or of what God requires. He often has a vivid sense of the particular ways in which men ignore, avoid, or disobey what is morally and religiously proper. His function is to lay bare the false pretenses of piety, the excessive certainty of pharisaic moralism, the optimistic claims of spirituality and personal sanctity, and the religious disguises in which human drives for power are clothed. He interprets the religious community's preoccupations with institutional success symbols and elaborate techniques for achieving institutional goals. He calls attention to failures to pursue the Church's properly defined mission. The prophet often is an acute observer of society and the movements that shape his historical period. He displays the potential human tragedies and disorder if certain policies are pursued, or if powerful groups are not checked. He uncovers subtle forms of injustice in the human community, through which men are suppressed and disinherited. He is the Church's ready representative against the powers of evil wherever they lurk.

Effective prophetic interpretation in the name of the Church requires clarity about the convictions out of which moral sensitivity and judgment grow. The prophet is strongly identified with the "true" God as against the "false" gods that claim the loyalties of the Church and the world. In another way, he is also strongly identified with the world; he is able to make clear the motives of men, and to judge the human consequences of their actions. His effectiveness for the community depends in part upon the perceptiveness of his interpretation of human events. If the prophet can see that to which others are blind, and if his portrayals and judgments prove to be accurate, he raises the level of esteem in which the world holds the Church. If he is heard in the Church and outside, and if reforming actions follow upon his judgments, his effect is a purification of the human community from some of its improprieties. The prophet functions as the Church's plumb line, in the light of which it measures the rectitude of its life and the life of the human community in general. The Church, a human community, needs its prophetic interpreters.

There are other interpreters in the Church. Historians interpret its past, and out of their work comes a new understanding of the community and its relation to contemporary movements and forces. Their work helps to maintain a consciousness of the continuing life of the community, and reminds it of both its past achievements and failures. Musicians interpret in their medium the texts of the Bible and the objects of the Church's belief. Their accomplishments may lead to a greater sense of unity of the congregations and to new means of religious experience. Laymen interpret their lives as members of the Christian community in relation to the requirements of their work and their leisure. The sense of unity and social identity in the Church is sustained and enhanced by various persons in various functions. The identity of the Church, with both its differentiation from, and affiliation with, other communities is clarified and preserved.

Every continuing historical community has its interpreters. As a human community, the Church participates in the same social process that other groups do. The nation's identity is expressed in certain key historical documents and traditions. To be kept alive, the meanings of these documents and traditions must be constantly interpreted in changing historical circumstances. Legislatures and courts develop the meaning of the national ethos and its charter documents in relation of various areas of social life. Teachers in the public schools interpret the meaning of the nation's signs in order to evoke a loyalty and understanding of its way of life. The problems of orthodoxy, heterodoxy, and heresy have their counterparts in the national life. Courts determine at what point an interpretation is so out of line with the charters and the moral consensus that it is subversive. The self-appointed preservers of national orthodoxy have social effects comparable to rigidly orthodox parties in the Church. Not only the nation, but other continuing communities are sustained by processes of interpretation.

The meanings that give identity to the various communities, however, are different. The final norms in the light of which each community's interpretations take place are different. The norms or "signs" of the communities are embodied in the ethos of each, and this ethos differs. The object of loyalty for each community—a person, a pattern of behavior, or a moral purpose—is different. Communities have different functions and different missions in the whole of human society.

The Church is not unique in being a community of interpretation, though all the particular offices to which the task is given do not have equivalent counterparts in other groups. Its differentiation rests in its final norm of interpretation. It has its own "sign," to use the language of Royce. The Bible carries its meanings and purposes: the Bible delineates its object of loyalty, God. It tells the story of the person who is the center of the Church's life, Jesus Christ. Creeds, ritual symbols, and liturgies function as "secondary signs"; they are relatively objective forms and patterns that bear potential meaning in the Church. The continuity and identity of the Church depend upon the effective interpretation of its signs; through interpretation they become meaningful for its members and to others. Interpretation is a community-creating and -sustaining process in the life of the Church.

CHAPTER 6

The Church: a Community of Memory and Understanding

The Christian Church has a "common memory." Its members have a common language for communication; the processes of interpretation extend the community and intensify the identification of its members with it. Through communication and interpretation the Church in any given time comes to know something about its life in the past, and particularly about the events most important in constituting and reforming it.

Part of the common memory of the Church is knowledge *about* the past; knowledge about the history of Israel, about Jesus Christ and the early Church, about St. Francis, the Reformation, the Puritans, John Wesley, and Alexander Campbell. The information needed for knowledge about the past life and important events of the Church is given in the Bible, the documents of the Church's history, the writings of theologians and preachers, and the works of Church historians. This information is available to anyone.

Knowledge about the constituting events and history of the Church, however, does not necessarily identify one subjectively with the Christian community. Men can have this knowledge without any internalization of its meaning, and thus without any significant identification with the Church. Knowledge about the Church is not the same as a subjective, personal identification with the meaning of the past events in the life of the Christian community.

The Possibility of Common Memory

The common memory of the community consists in a subjective understanding of its past; each of its members in the present relives the meanings of past events in its history, and makes them part of his personal history. Common memory involves an empathetic participation in the history of the community through the stories and other expressions of past events. Members of the Church in the present time grasp, understand, and identify themselves with the meanings of events recorded and interpreted in the Bible, Christian symbols, and other representations. Events in the life of the community, and the community's understanding of the meaning of these events, have been objectified or expressed in literature, liturgies, architecture, and art. These expressions are the media through which the community in the present understands and relives the past.[1]

The Bible, for example, is a meaningful interpretation of historical events. It becomes a medium through which men in the present can project themselves into these events and their meanings and thus be

---

[1] Perhaps any aesthetically sensitive or imaginative historian can understand, relive, and re-create, as if from within, the past events in the life of the Church. He is not necessarily *committed* to these events as normative for understanding himself and human history. The element of commitment is a further differentiation between belonging and not belonging to the Christian community, and will be dealt with in the following chapter.

subjectively identified with the past. The meanings conveyed by the Biblical writers become significant for the personal existence of contemporary Christians and their Church. The Bible guides the understanding of the formative events and their meanings for the Church in all historical periods.[2]

Common memory makes possible common life. Many persons share the same meaningful events, each as a part of his own personal history. Men are drawn together through the common meanings they share as personally significant for each and for the community. The members of the Christian community know one person, and the events of which he was a part, to provide the reason for the existence of the Church. Jesus Christ, meaningfully interpreted in the life of the Church, becomes the point of integration of life and meanings for individual Christians and their community. To be sure, not all members of congregations testify to Christ as the integrating meaning for their lives. To the extent that other centers are more dominant, a person's identification with the Church is weaker, and consequently the common life is weaker.

The community keeps its common memory alive by continually rehearsing the important events of its history. The reading of the Bible is one means by which Christians understand and relive the past. The Church Year in the worship life of the community is a dramatic presentation of the history of the most significant events surrounding Jesus

[2] The reflections of the present chapter began upon reading H. R. Niebuhr's *The Meaning of Revelation*, New York, 1941, pp. 110 ff. The expansion of the theme has been guided by the writings of a number of philosophers and theologians. Josiah Royce, in *The Problem of Christianity*, particularly Vol. II, pp. 1-55, develops the significance of common memory and common hope for any community, and particularly the Christian Church. The continuation of a common memory is possible because the community interprets life in the light of a "sign" that continues through history. The past is made contemporary for a community as persons make its events a part of their personal histories. Cf. J. H. Cotton, *Royce on the Human Self*, Cambridge, Mass., 1954.

The theme of time and community developed by Royce is in part a social extension of St. Augustine's understanding of the function of memory and aspiration for the self as he expresses it in the *Confessions*, Book XI. For Augustine selfhood exists essentially in the moment, but in relation to memory and anticipation. Indeed, as the *Confessions* indicates, the self's understanding of itself finds coherence in the meaning of a past experience, i.e., the conversion in Augustine's case. Royce also deals with the importance of memory and hope for individuality.

A more existentialist interpretation of how a self and a community can be related to the past can be developed with reference to the process of *Verstehen*, or "interpretive understanding." Max Weber's interpretation of this method can be found particularly in *The Theory of Social and Economic Organization*, New

Christ: Advent as the expectation of his coming to rule, Christmas as the celebration of his birth, Lent as preparation for the rehearsal of the events of his Passion, Death, and Resurrection. Protestants rehearse their especially cherished historical event, the beginning of the Reformation. Feast Days and Saints Days in the Catholic churches have a similar function.

Subjective understanding comes through remembering and reliving the past. Christians gain not only knowledge about the past, but in a sense participate in the past life of the Church. The self participates in the meaningful history of the Church, and comes to interpret and understand itself in the light of these meanings. The meaning of the past is internalized. The same past is internalized by many. In these processes the sense of common purpose and life grows, and the identity of persons with the historical community is deepened. Continuity of an inner community, and the sense of an inner unity, exist through common memory.

The Bible and the Church's Inner Unity and Continuity

Continuity of memory is based in part upon continuity of the lived experience of Christians through the centuries. Continuity of experience in turn is based upon the function of the Bible in the history of the Church. Events that were meaningful in the first century can be meaningful in the present because they are recorded and interpreted in the Bible. Experiences of men in the time of the primitive Church can inform contemporary understanding and experience because they have been expressed in the Bible. The deeply subjective, existential continuity of the Christian community has been possible because of the Bible.

The Bible has this significance because it is the record of the lived

---

York, 1947, pp. 88-112. Weber defines a method of knowing for the cultural sciences that can describe the subjective meaning of human action.

In Weber's intellectual background is the work of Wilhelm Dilthey. The present chapter relies heavily on his analysis, which can be found in various essays, but particularly in *Gesammelte Schriften*, Vol. VII, Leipzig and Berlin, 1927, pp. 191-251, where he outlines a "Critique of Historical Reason." The lived experience (*Erlebnis*) of persons and communities is objectified or expressed in art, philosophy, religion, and other aspects of culture. This experience can be understood, relived, and reconstructed by a projection of the self through the objective expressions into the past. Dilthey sought to define a method of knowing appropriate to the human or cultural studies. I am not concerned here about the validity of his method for science, but rather wish to show that what he describes takes place in the normal processes of Church life. See the Appendix of this book for a further discussion of time and community.

experience of early Christians, and the meaning of the person and event of Jesus Christ. In order to understand either the Bible, or the primitive Christian experience, or Jesus Christ, the other two must be brought into view. The Bible expresses the meaning of the Jesus Christ who brought the community into being, and gave it its identity. It is the record of the constituting events, and their meanings for Christians; thus it provides the center of identity of the Church in all times. In order to understand the Bible one must understand the lived experience of the early Church, and the event that brought it into being. In order to understand the experience of the early Church one must understand the constituting event and therefore the record of both in the Bible. And in order to understand the person Jesus Christ one must know what he meant in the experience of early Christians, and therefore the Bible. The three are interrelated in themselves. Continuity of both the meaning of the person Jesus Christ and the experience of Christians is grounded in the function of the Bible in the Church.

The Church, however, must go behind the New Testament in order to understand it. The continuity of ethos in the Christian community extends back into the life and history of Israel. The early Church interpreted Jesus Christ, its center of meaning, in the light of the signs and expressions of the people of Israel. Just as the Church now understands its ethos by a rehearsal of its past, so the early Christians understood Jesus Christ through the memories of Israel's history and expectations. The early Church did not remember simply a chronology of events from previous centuries, or the narratives of heroic deeds. The experience and history of the Jews had a religious importance; it was a meaningful history, and a history of meanings. Events were described not only with reference to what in fact occurred, but also to the religious and moral significance of what occurred. The Jews in Jesus' time were existentially engaged in their history. There was an ethos of religious meaning that was expressed in the actions and events of life and in their interpretation. Jesus came into a community of memory; the lived experience of his people was expressed in the Old Testament. These writings in turn became the basis for understanding Jesus and later events. Thus the community of memory and understanding is continuous between Jews and Christians.

The events around Jesus Christ took place in a community with its particular history and meanings. He and his followers shared the ethos of the Jews. This ethos entered into the actions of Jesus and into the understanding and interpretation of them by others. The Gospel narratives give ample evidence of this. The existence of this ethos, shared by Jesus and his followers, made possible an inner receptiveness in the disciples, Paul, and others. The continuity with the Jewish ethos made possible the loyalty out of which a new community could emerge. But Jesus Christ as person and event had his own existence; new meanings came into life within the old. The new meanings from the new event are expressed in the New Testament. They continued to be interpreted and understood, however, within the context of the memory of the Jews. The center of the new community is understood with reference to the memory of events in the old. There is no absolute discontinuity of memory even though the New Testament is an expression of the lived experience of a new community coming into being around a particular historical event. What is expressed in the New Testament carries with it the living past of the community into which Jesus Christ came.

The Church is obviously not absolutely determined by Israel. In the light of the new center of meaning, Jesus Christ, the significance of past events was changed. Those who became disciples of Jesus in the flesh, and those who knew him through the experience of others, had a different lived experience from the other Jews. Through their new loyalty certain aspects of the history of the old community were revised in their importance. For example, the moral and cultic law had a different status and significance, as one sees both in the gospel accounts of Jesus' ministry (e.g., "Man was not made for the Sabbath. . . .") and in Paul's epistles. Events in the past were understood to foreshadow the event that constituted the Church. Jesus Christ had come "in the fulness of time." That which preceded, now had a new importance, for it had prepared the way. The memory of the past took a new shape and purpose in the light of the present lived experience of the early Christians.

The anticipations of the future also changed. The Church's expectations of the future were deeply influenced by the expectations of the Jews, but Jewish hopes had to be revised in the light of the lived experience of Jesus Christ. The meaning of the new life cast the hope into a new mold. The Church's expectation, like its memory, was continuous with that of the Jews, though not absolutely determined by it. Jesus Christ now became the focal point for understanding what the future meant, and what it had in store.

The Bible is the receptacle of meaning in which the possibility exists of a common memory and hope throughout the Church's history. Its own texts are examples of how a common memory informed the historical particularity and continuity of a people. They remembered Moses, the Exodus, David, and the prophets. Jesus had to be understood in relation to this past and to the hopes that were forthcoming from it. The Biblical accounts continue to be the basis of a continuity of memory and hope between the present Church and the past. The present generation can be "contemporaneous with Christ" because the Bible expresses his person and what he meant in the early Church. The importance of Jesus Christ is expressed for the past and the future, as well as for present experience. The history of Israel is seen as a preparation for Jesus Christ, and for contemporary experience of him. The accounts of Christian expectations and hope give an understanding of the cosmic and ultimate significance of Jesus Christ. Personal life, in its memory and hope, is illumined by an understanding of Jesus Christ. Common life is understood in the light of the past, and in the expectation of the Kingdom of God.

The Bible, as the expression of the meaning of Jesus Christ and the experience of the early Church, continues to be the most important historical object that marks the Church. It is an objective expression of the common meaning that is the inner mark of the Christian community. The identity and continuity of the Church as a community of persons depends upon the continued rehearsal, understanding, and reliving of the past expressed in the Bible. The continuation of Jesus Christ as the center of meaning that differentiates the Church from other groups requires a continuous interpretation and understanding of the present and the future in the light of this past. An understanding of the Church requires an understanding of the Bible; an understanding of the Bible requires an understanding of the Church. To understand these two one must understand the significance of Jesus Christ, and what he meant in the life of the early Christians. The three cannot be separated in an interpretation of the Church.[3]

The lived experience of the Church at any time is evoked by a confrontation of a generation or group with the meaning of Jesus Christ as it is expressed in the lived experience of the early Church and re-

---

[3] The same process takes place in the national community and other groups. Events with crucial meaning for the nation are expressed in historical texts and documents, and other objective signs. The continuation of the spirit or ethos of a nation requires the continued rehearsal of these events and meanings that mark the national identity. E.g., the American Revolution functions similarly to the event of Jesus Christ in the Church in its importance for the American people. Or, the identity of the American South as a culture depends upon the rehearsal of events in the decades 1840-70.

corded in the Bible. The community lives as it continually apprehends the meanings of its constituting event, and responds to it. The inner life of the Church is never self-created in a particular time and place; it does not make it own norms of belief and conduct; it is not the 'master of its own life. Rather it is the contemporary form of life in relation to Jesus Christ. This person and event are expressed uniquely in the Bible. Jesus Christ could not be the continuing center around which identity and meaning of action take place in the Church apart from the words, stories, and concepts of the Bible. Each generation appropriates the event which created the community through an understanding of the Bible.

The memory of Jesus Christ is common and deeply personal insofar as it becomes the center of meaning that gives coherence to the personal existence of the various members of the Church. The meaning of Jesus Christ is not a museum piece preserved for interest in archaisms; it is personally apprehended by the members of the Church as it illumines their own existence. The sense of inner community felt by Christians rests in a common quality of lived experience. This in turn rests in the common memory of a past event, Jesus Christ. The common memory is possible because the Bible objectively bears the record of the person and meanings that give identity and continuity to the deepest common experiences of Christians.

Holy Communion and Common Memory

The Bible is not the only bearer of the possibility of common memory and meaning in the Church. In many of its rites the Church reminds its members of the past. Services for the consecration of marriage remind the couple and congregation of Jesus' participation in the wedding feast at Cana; services of baptism recall the baptism of Jesus, and his calling of little children to come to him. The figure of the cross, and other Christian symbols, are visual reminders of the past and its meaning. Of particular significance is the celebration of Holy Communion, which is a dramatization of the meaning of a past event in which Christians in the present participate. Communion has at least a twofold social function: it rehearses actions instituted by Jesus Christ, and it identifies Christians in the present with their fellow believers of all times and places.

The New Testament records the occasion of the Last Supper, at which Jesus broke bread with his disciples and gave the elements their religious significance. Bread and wine are representations of Jesus

Christ, and particularly of the meaning of his suffering and death. The celebration rehearses the passion and death of Christ. It reconstitutes within the community a memory of its constituting events. The words of institution, taken from I Corinthians 11, call attention to the occasion at which the supper was first celebrated, "that the Lord Jesus on the night when he was betrayed. . . ." The action rehearses and revives the memory of Good Friday, "This is my body which is broken for you"; "this cup is the new covenant in my blood." The meanings expressed are not significant for their objective historical value, but only as they are personally true for those who believe. His body is broken *"for* you," and his blood shed *"for* the remission of sin." Objective historical facts of a broken body and shed blood do not in themselves constitute and revive a social group. The meaning of the occasion for the community, dramatically rehearsed, creates and sustains social identity and continuity. Further, the words of institution report Jesus as saying, "This do in remembrance of me." Christians project themselves into the situation of the eve of Good Friday, they relive the significance of the death of Christ through its representations in the substance of bread and wine and the action of the celebration. Holy Communion renews the inner identity of the Church with Jesus Christ, its center of meaning.

Holy Communion is socially important also because through it a congregation identifies itself with the whole Church, past and present. The common celebration of this event through history and across the nations is recalled. Through participation one is identified with the disciples in the Upper Room, the Pauline congregations of the first century, medieval and Reformation Christians, and the Christians in the history of a particular denomination. The present dramatic action evokes the memory of the celebration of the supper throughout the history of the Church. The believer is identified with Christians in other denominations, those in oppressed churches under hostile governments, and those in the younger churches, for all remember and relive a common event; all share a common memory. Protestantism's institutionalization of "World-Wide Communion Sunday" is a modern effort to encourage the sense of oneness in the Church through the celebration of Holy Communion.

Holy Communion is a representation of a significant event in the emergence of the Church. Christians of all times and places have come to share the meaning of the event, and through the service of Communion can remember and relive it. What is relived is common to all Christians: the meaning of the death of Jesus; it is important to Christians as individuals for it forms the center of their belief and piety. In the rehearsal and its meaning the identification of both individuals and churches with Jesus Christ and with other Christians is renewed and sustained. All Christians share the same history; it is existentially important both to their personal lives and to their life together.

Holy Communion is significant to all Christians. Like baptism, preaching, and some form of ministry, it is only slightly less important than the Bible. Like the Bible and other aspects of Church life, however, Communion is both unifying and divisive. It represents a common center of meaning, but also highly particularized interpretations of this meaning. Consequently, it is socially not only unifying and integrative, but also differentiating and disintegrative. The closer a representation is to the meaning of the central person and event in the Church, the more important it is. Its great importance makes it the object of detailed interpretations and specific definitions of meaning. What is most common to the whole community becomes most socially divisive. Theological discussion has historically been extensive and intensive on the question of Communion because of its acknowledged universal importance. This discussion, like all theological discussion, has fostered both unity and division in the Church. The emphasis on the meaning of Communion during the decades of the Reformation illustrates its theological significance and also its socially divisive power. Continuity and discontinuity in the social unity of the Church can both be traced to Communion, the bearer of potential common memory. Its place in contemporary ecumenical discussions both in the World Council of Churches and between particular churches like the Church of England and the Church of Scotland, continues to manifest its social significance.

Church History and Continuity

Among the other actions and activities of the Church that are important for the common memory is the writing and study of Church history. The history of the church can be written and read with two different but proper intentions. One is to re-create and restore as objectively as possible all the data relevant to the whole history of the Church, or to a special aspect of it. This involves research and interpretation, relating sets of data to each other in the sequence of events narrated. Reading Church history written in this manner brings a store of information about the past life of the Christian community.

Events can be placed in proper chronological order, and be seen in relation to corresponding events in general history.

The other intention in writing and reading Church history is to re-create the story of the life and thought of the community in such a way as to foster an understanding of its inner dynamic. The reader can understand what the events meant to the actors, and what their meaningful implications are for later developments. The history of the Church becomes not only an external collection of data, but an inner understanding of the meaning of events that have shaped the community. The reader not only develops a factual ordering of data; he can project himself into the history. He can see its significance not only for the Church in a particular past time and place, but for the present as well. In this way the identification with the past, through its moments of great consequence for the Church, becomes inner and subjective in character. The history is inwardly appropriated.

Common Past and Common Present

Through the processes of communication, interpretation, and subjective understanding, the Church in the present is continuous with the Church through history. Its identity and continuity are preserved and extended. The Bible, sacraments, preaching, creeds, symbols, and Church history are all objectifications of the lived experience of the community in earlier periods. Through these the members of the Church in the present project themselves into the inner experiences and meanings of earlier years. There is a center of meaning that gives consensus to the Church in any age, and binds the community together through time. This center is in a person, an event, Jesus Christ, who has been meaningfully interpreted and objectified in the Bible and other forms.

Continuity in the Church as an historical community is grounded in the continuity of a center of meaning that differentiates the Church from other historical societies, e.g., the French nation, the Freemasons, or Western culture. Social continuity and identity in the Church depend upon the continued significance of this center, Jesus Christ, with his manifold meanings, for contemporary persons and churches. Continuity exists not only for the preservation of an ancient truth. The lived experience of the past that was important enough to be remembered and expressed has contemporary significance as well. The present memory of Jesus Christ is not the admiration of an antique; it is a reliving in the present of his meaningfulness. Jesus Christ continues to provide a center for personal integrity and social consensus. The Christian's "contemporaneity with Christ" occurs throughout the history of the Church. It is possible because Christ has continued to be a powerful center of integration of experience through history. The one who was the Church's center of life through centuries continues to provide the center of life in the present. The one who was a personal center of meaning to Paul, Augustine, Francis, Luther, Rauschenbusch, and many individuals long lost to history continues to be a personal center of meaning to church leaders who will be remembered and to thousands of believers who will be forgotten.

The Church's continuity and identity, then, is maintained both by a remembering and reliving of the past, and by the present power and significance of meanings from the past. The past and present flow into each other: The Church looks to the past for insight into the present; the present situation of the Church gives special insight into certain aspects of its history. The Church returns to the Bible and crucial patterns of common life in order to judge its present state and to inform its present actions. The present life of the Church also evokes the memory of particular aspects of the past.

Reformation in the Church is always the double process of a normative past becoming meaningful in the present, and a present crisis finding illumination from the past. Reformation is a renewed subjective understanding of past meanings as they enlighten present issues, and of the actions that are consequent from this. The past becomes meaningful in the present. What is remembered is relived, but never explicitly as it was first lived. For example, Luther's appropriation of the New Testament was a complex process. Both a personal crisis of faith and a social crisis in the Church evoked an effort to find a living meaning in Jesus Christ. The reliving, however, was no simple duplication of the experiences recorded in the gospels and epistles; it was an expression in the sixteenth-century situation of the meaning of an event recorded in the New Testament in the first century. The meaning was relived not only because it belonged to the early Church, but because it was self-validating in the light it shed on the plight of man and the Church in Luther's time. As St. Paul had to relate life under the gospel to the legalism of the Judaizing Christians, Luther had to relate it to the works-righteousness of Catholicism.

Reformation is a social necessity. Renewed understanding of the center of meaning that gives identity to the Church is required if that identity is to persist. The ideas of a particular reformer must become a conviction for others if the reformation is to be effective. He must persuade others that by the return to the meaning of Jesus Christ the life of the Church will be properly rectified and revived.[4]

The continuity of particular Christian groups requires the same process as the continuity of the whole Church. Protestants remember Luther and Calvin, and to some extent seek to find the appropriate contemporary expressions of their reforming work. Lutherans reform their own particular tradition by a return to Luther. One sees this taking place in the Luther research of scholars in Europe and in America. Some American Congregationalists look to seventeenth-century Puritanism for an expression of church and social life that can be re-expressed in the present decades, just as some Methodists would return to John Wesley.

The Christian community is in part divided by what is remembered and relived. Churches are separated by their particular understandings of what is the appropriate contemporary expression of common life in Jesus Christ. In short, social divisions are the result of separate interpretations of Jesus Christ and his significance, or divisions of meaning. Opposing parties in the Church have existed from the first century. St. Paul struggled with the problem of whether the meaning of Jesus Christ had to be restricted to its Judaic context and expressions. In the Pauline churches parties arose over interpretations, and centered around particular interpreters—Paul, Cephas, Apollo. The gospels carry their own unique expressions of meaning as well as a common center of identity: Matthew especially relates Jesus to the Jewish tradition, Luke is fascinated with the extraordinary and miraculous, John uses the language of Hellenistic culture.

The various expressions of the meaning of Jesus Christ are relative to their interpreters and the situations they address. This is so in the New Testament and continues to be so in the Church's history. Certain aspects of the meaning of Jesus Christ and the community-creating events are existentially more pertinent to particular personal, ecclesiastical, or social situations. Certain aspects of common memory are stressed under special conditions. Particular expressions have become normative for particular churches and movements. A particular aspect of the common memory often becomes the point of reference for a new Christian group.

---

[4] This paragraph reflects a Protestant viewpoint. In Catholicism, both Roman and Eastern, the unbroken chain of tradition is cherished. Continuity of development with constant reference to particular theologians and events from the past is more characteristic than reformation.

The identity of a group persists as long as its special expressions remain normative for it; that is, as long as they are remembered and relived. For example, Pietists believed that Jesus Christ was best understood if the Church emphasized personal religious experience of sin and regeneration, the devotional life, and a rigid line between the saved and the unsaved. The distinctive identity of a particular pietistic denomination is maintained as long as these expressions continue to be meaningful for its members. When they are no longer the garments of contemporary church life, the inner identity of the group fades. There is lamenting on the part of some for the loss of the old-time religion. If the group loses its consensus it must struggle to find a new one, or die.

The meaning of Jesus Christ, as the one who gives unity to the whole Church, is always related to particular persons, communities, and cultures. The common center finds special expressions in relation to the lived experience of particular persons or the values of particular cultures. The Church's history is the story of its effort to preserve the common locus of identity while finding those particular expressions of its significance that are appropriate to special times and places. The Church always has a problem of consistency. It must relate Jesus Christ to persons and a society dominated in one place by Hinduism, in another by secular democracy, in another by primitive religion. The problem is one suggested earlier: To what extent are particular expressions so closely identified with the meaning of Jesus Christ that he is lost in the absence of these words, concepts, and images? Christians are socially divided by their solutions to this problem. The problem may be stated more radically: To what extent is the very meaning of Jesus Christ so bound to the history and culture in which he appeared that it cannot be universalized without universalizing elements of that culture and history? How can the culturally conditioned expressions of meaning from one time and place be the vehicles for appropriation of the same meaning in another time and place without distorting the meaning itself? The Church in recent decades has been asked this question by historians like Troeltsch and Bultmann.

From the point of view of a social interpretation of the Church, the relating process is to some extent an inherently relativizing one. What one group remembers and relives is affected by the personal and cultural context in which the process of understanding goes on. The relating is necessary if Jesus Christ is to be personally meaningful to a particular people (or if the past is to be existentially present). It does not, however, entail a complete relativization; there is a fairly consistent expression of the meaning of the Church's knowledge of God in the Bible, the creeds, the sacraments, and other "objectifications." These insure in a broad way that it is Jesus Christ who is understood and remembered. The great importance of objective expressions can be seen at this point: they offer the possibility of a common inner community of Christians. They at least set the outer limits beyond which a community becomes "non-Christian." Further, the Church does the interpreting; Jesus Christ who is interpreted is the center of life for the persons and community in which the processes of understanding go on. The relativization is limited by continuity at two levels—the objective expressions and the community itself.

The processes of understanding that preserve the inner continuity and unity of the Church also function in other communities. A nation has an ethos expressed in documents, historical events, and many types of monuments. It is kept alive and revived by various types of rehearsals of the past—civic celebrations, flags, pledges of loyalty, stories, pictures, and education. Persons are more deeply identified with a nation if its center of meaning informs their own outlooks. If a center that contradicts that of the nation is important to a person, his participation in the national community is marginal. Disputes arise over the orthodoxy, heterodoxy, and heresy of various expressions of the meaning of national life. There is a selectivity of meaning in the nation related to particular needs of persons and to particular historical situations.

The processes of understanding, remembering, and reliving are part of the natural world; they are possible because of the nature of man. Differentiation between the Christian community and, e.g., the nation, cannot be made according to the nature of the processes by which the communities continue to exist. The difference lies in what meanings are remembered, understood, relived, and newly expressed. The same processes serve different meanings and values. Each community has its own objective expressions of what it believes and stands for. Jesus Christ is quite a different person from George Washington or Abraham Lincoln. The events out of which the Church came into being have a different meaning from the events out of which the American nation came. The Church is characterized by its unique objective center of meaning, Jesus Christ, carried in its appropriate expressions, and internalized in the Church. The Church is the community that remembers Jesus Christ, understands what he means, relives this meaning, and gives it contemporary expression in personal and common life.

CHAPTER 7

The Church:
a Community of Belief and Action

The Church is a community of belief and action. Persons will and decide to belong to it, or to remain in it. They are committed to its object of belief. They self-consciously confess and acknowledge their membership. They are impelled to act in the light of their loyalty. It is a moral community. The Church is a covenanted community; not merely a natural community.[1]

A common distinction is made between "natural" and "organic" communities on the one hand, and "associational" or "covenanted" communities on the other. For example, in political theory there are those who have interpreted the nation primarily in terms of common cultural and linguistic characteristics, and those who have understood it primarily in relation to the state as the outgrowth of a process of rationally determined social contract. A more mechanistic analogy tends to prevail in contract theories; the whole is assumed to be made up of its individual parts placed in relation to one another. Relations are assumed to be more external than internal in character. The political theory of John Locke is of this type. It is similar to a "covenant" understanding of the Church at least insofar as a commitment rationally made and bound by a group of persons is involved. In contrast, an organic view of society may be more characteristic of Romantic social and political theorists (in contrast to the contractual views of the Enlightenment). Society is seen to be more than the sum of its parts; the parts are interdependent as are the parts of the body. Relations are internal in character. A Biblical example of an interpretation of Christians in this language is found in I Corinthians 12. In the last three chapters we have used a framework in which the Church was seen as a natural development of

[1] In this chapter I will not deal with the theological interpretation of covenant; i.e., that the covenant is initiated by God. Theologically understood, God covenants with a people; the community is not merely the result of a social contract freely engaged in by persons. My concern continues to be, however, an interpretation of the Church as a social and human community from the "manward" side.

F. W. Dillistone's *The Structure of the Divine Society*, London, 1951. interprets the Church in the light of "organic" and "covenant" conceptions.

a more or less organic type. But the Church cannot be understood properly if we limit ourselves to this view. The two types are not mutually exclusive; indeed they are necessary to each other in Church as well as in nation.

Every person participates in many communities to which he has not pledged allegiance in a self-conscious manner. The outlook of a contemporary American, for example, is shaped not only by the Constitution, which he may have had occasion to acknowledge in an oath. It is also shaped by his internalization of meanings and values communicated by mass advertising and entertainment, or by the ethos of a particular region or village. Symbols of group membership function without awareness of the process by which one becomes identified with them. The American suburbanite does not pledge himself to join and be faithful to the suburban way of life, and to use it as a basis for his personal existence and social outlook. He makes no confession of faith in this pattern of life with its implicit commitments to certain definitions of the right, the good, and the ultimate effective powers. Indeed, he may not seek membership in this community intentionally; he may just begin to act and look like a suburbanite through the natural processes of socialization. Self-consciousness of personal identification with a way of life may come only when one observes another way in the role of the stranger, or when the way is threatened by other forces, or when it is objectified and criticized by the social observer and moral prophet. Identification with the Church comes partly in the same way as identification with the suburban way of life, or the Chinese way of life, or that of any community of meaning and value. But there is more to social identification than this.

Identification with the Church has also involved an act of covenanting, or something similar to it. At some point the Christian acknowledges and confesses that he belongs to the Church and is loyal to its center of life, Jesus Christ. The precise nature of this act of acknowledgment and commitment is an important point of dispute in the Church, and thus a point at which social divisions are defined. For some the act of infant baptism, with no self-conscious awareness on the part of the child, appears to suffice; for others baptism must be complemented by an act of confirmation. For some a personal religious experience expressed in a testimony and a promise of loyalty is necessary; for others religious experience must be accompanied by right doctrinal belief and proper moral behavior. In a time of Church crisis, as in the church struggle in Germany in the 1930's, a clearer confession may be required than in a time of relative social freedom, peace, and prosperity. The forms of acknowledgment and commitment vary. But from the human side (without engaging in a doctrinal discussion of the priority of grace, or the extent of human co-operation in election), the Church can be said to be a community of commitment, or covenant, as well as a natural community. It is a community of *confessed* belief and faith in Jesus Christ, the object which marks its historic distinctiveness; it is not only a community of internalized general Christian meanings. It is also a "community of *deed*"; there are common actions forthcoming from belonging to the Church. It is a community of acknowledged loyalty to a person and a pattern of meanings.[2]

The Church is not socially unique by virtue of being a community of committed loyalty, belief, and action. Other communities also take a covenanted form; they are given their shapes both by the processes of internalization of meaning, and the self-conscious acknowledgment of, and commitment to, a particular pattern of truth and order of values. The act of covenant or joining involves common elements in various societies, whether it be a trade union, the 4-H Club, or the Church. Particular churches resemble particular nonreligious social organizations. For example, in most American denominations the joining process is similar to that of other voluntary associations. By contrast, for Scandinavian Lutheranism, baptism and even confirmation do not have the decisiveness of a voluntary intentional act and commitment. The secular counterpart of national churches is more clearly the nation-state than the voluntary association. One is born a citizen of the nation, and received by baptism as a member of the church; one has duties to both, and both render services to the person throughout his life. A special act is required to leave rather than to join the church. Nevertheless, while different from the commitment required by a gathered or voluntary church, baptism and particularly confirmation imply an assent that has social consequences.

Voluntary joining does not of itself, however, insure an intense conviction about the truth to which a person commits himself. Sectarianism in its classical Troeltschian sense has had a vision of the Church as a

---

[2] Many writers have dealt with the double character of human societies, and particularly religious societies. The present chapter is indebted among others to F. Toennies, *Gemeinschaft und Gesellschaft*, 2nd ed., Berlin, 1912; Royce, *The Problem of Christianity*, Vol. II, and *The Philosophy of Loyalty*, New York, 1908. Existentialist discussions of "inwardness," "seriousness," and "faith" have affected the character of this chapter, particularly the argument of Kierkegaard's *Concluding Unscientific Postscript*, Princeton, 1948.

community of restored, believing, disciplined Christians. The act of joining has decisively marked the Christian's life into two periods, and his social participation into two spheres. Tests of eligibility have been more or less charitably administered in screening the worthy from the unworthy. But the historic dilemma of sects in the second and third generation indicates a double social option. Either they lower the requirements for membership (with a consequent effect of weakening the intensity of group identification), or they observe an exodus from the group by those birthright participants who do not meet the requirements for formal initiation into the group. The former option seems to be historically most commonly exercised, and thus one observes churches founded on a strict covenant principle existing with *pro forma* covenants. The communal discipline weakens, whether exercised by external authority (because of a surrender of personal autonomy in the act of joining) or by the inner consciences and wills of the members. Thus there is no necessary correlation between externally observable membership, and intensity of inner commitment and belief in a sect or "free church" denomination. Comparably in a folk church, the absence of the decisive act of free covenanting does not mean that intensity of commitment and belief cannot take place in this less voluntaristic society.

As a consequence, an analysis of the elements of commitment, belief, and corporate action cannot be pursued with reference only to the external forms of church membership. No absolutely accurate boundaries can be externally perceived that are identical with an inner community of belief, commitment, and action. There are differences in intensity and extensity of belief and action. The same members differ from time to time in self-consciousness of their loyalty to the Church and to Jesus Christ. Neither degrees of belief and commitment nor the precise extent of participation in corporate action are measurable.

The Community of Belief

The Christian community is defined at some point by those who say, "I believe in Jesus Christ." The meaning of Jesus Christ is variously defined in the variety of creeds and personal confessions, but at some point membership in the Church is acknowledged and confessed in terms of loyalty to him. A voluntary act, either in acknowledgment of an inner truth believed, or in submission to ecclesiastical authority, marks one's participation in the Church. The confession may be, on the one hand, an expression of the living faith and experience of the individual and the community; it may be a confession of a subjective truth. On the other hand, the confession may be a formal acknowledgment of what is believed to be an objectively true statement about God, Jesus Christ, and the Church. In this instance the believer may be willfully submitting himself to an externally authoritative statement of belief, the historic belief of the Church, rather than expressing his own belief. Or the two may be joined: what the Church has claimed to be true may be inwardly believed to be true.

The Church has a body of beliefs that distinguishes it from other human communities. These are expressed in the creeds and confessions of the Church. They vary from extensive and elaborate definitions of the object of belief to minimal statements such as "I believe in Jesus Christ as Lord." Giving assent to the beliefs of the Church is part of belonging to the Christian community. Divisions in the community occur around such questions as what expression of belief is most accurate and adequate, and what is the *sine qua non* of belief that marks one a member of the Church. But at some point a member gives quiet assent to, if not public confession of, his acceptance of the object of belief, and therefore to at least a minimal belief system.

In the Church, however, belief implies more than intellectual assent. It implies trust, faith, commitment, loyalty, and obedience in and to the object of belief. These aspects of the Church's common life are more peculiar to its existence than others, and therefore are more difficult to account for in the language of social interpretation. Yet there are analogues to faith, trust, commitment, loyalty, and obedience in other human communities as well. Members of the Christian community, in varying degrees and differing from time to time, trust the community's object of belief. In Jesus Christ they find the person and meanings on which they rely in life and death. For Christians, Jesus Christ gives meaning to the ultimate reality, and to the experience of men in relation to God. The Church, then, is a community of faith; a community that relies on Jesus Christ as the revelation of the knowledge and power most adequate for living, and for understanding God and human life before God.

Nations and ideological communities are also communities of faith. While most Americans, for example, would find it difficult to defend intellectually their assent and commitment to democracy, they nonetheless trust in it as an adequate and meaningful basis for social life. Membership in the American community is determined in a large measure by one's acceptance of democracy as a basis for political and social life. To have faith in a radically different basis of life is to be separated from the American community, informally if not formally. The assent given in daily participation may on occasion be publicly confessed. Dispute occurs over what definition of the American belief system is an adequate expression of the common life, or of the objective truths that give shape to the nation. Definitions acceptable to most university professors, for example, were not acceptable to Senator Joseph McCarthy of Wisconsin. The extent to which public and detailed confessions of American faith are required for formal membership and the enjoyment of the rights and privileges of membership has been a matter of debate. As in the Church, so in the nation there are those who stress inner trust and confidence more than they do a detailed confession of loyalty. As in the Church, so in the nation there is no necessary correlation between a verbally articulated statement of belief and the inner convictions that inform and guide life. Whether inner commitment is sufficient, or whether it must be joined with frequent verbal confession, is a matter of dispute. Nevertheless, more inclusive than the disputes is the acceptance of some articles of belief as a basis for national membership, whether this be done implicitly or explicitly. There is an expression of confidence in the meanings and truths on which the national life rests.

Some ideological communities require more orthodoxy than others just as some Christian groups require more detailed confessions than others. The analogies between Christian zeal in sectarianism and Communist zeal in the party cells have been drawn frequently in recent decades. Communist beliefs function comparably to belief in Jesus Christ as a basis for personal integrity and social identification. The surrender of autonomy to the authority of the human leader or the group's consensus, however, has few recent historical counterparts in Protestant churches. Certainly the authoritative "change of party line" has no clear counterparts in the Church. The Church is a more mature and secure community; even its most creedal forms leave room for diversity of opinion on points considered to be of secondary importance. The absolute unanimity in detail that characterizes the highly disciplined Communist Party cell is inherently in conflict with the meanings believed in the Christian Church, though Christian groups have from time to time desired and sought such power.

In the processes of communication, interpretation, and understanding the past, it is possible to be influenced by the meanings of the Christian community without being committed to them. Western Culture, through the media of art, poetry, and music, for example, is informed by the events out of which the Church came into being and is brought to a recollection of them. But this takes places without the necessity of *belief* in the meanings. A Bach Passion Chorale, a Rouault figure of Christ, or Auden's "Christmas Oratorio" may be interpreted and understood, at least in part, without specific reference to either the religious beliefs of the author, the interpreter, or the audience. The Bible has affected the language of various nations and informed a general moral consensus within the human community. But the general cultural community does not consequently *seek* in Jesus Christ, or in the Bible, an illumination of the nature of God, or of the human situation, or of the power of hope and renewal. The Christian community in a more restricted sense consists of those who not only know what the Church and Jesus Christ mean, but also inwardly believe them to be true. It is a community of those committed to these meanings, finding in them an authentication of life as it is before God, and seeking in them knowledge of both the power and the goodness that rules the world.

Members of the Church seek both self-understanding and an understanding of events in the world in the light of Jesus Christ. This person, and the meanings carried by the Church, are, of course, not the only sources of self-understanding. It involves knowledge of the psychological, physiological, and sociological determinants of life. There have been Christians who reduced all these to matters of religious meaning, but the limited sufficiency of the Church's beliefs to give a causal explanation of personal events and experiences has been acknowledged in a number of ways. Various doctrines of the autonomy of nature have permitted supplementary explanations of events. But natural causal explanations do not exhaust the issues of life. Christians seek not only causes, or even one unifying cause; they also seek to understand the moral, human, and religious significance of personal existence. Elements of meaning are found not only in viewing the self as natural, but by understanding the self in relation to God through the meanings carried by the Church. Christians seek and find understanding in the center of meaning of the Christian community, Jesus Christ. Commitment in and through the Church gives a person a center of life in common with others. He trusts God through these meanings. God is the object to which they ultimately point. Trust is no mere casual occurrence; it involves belief, and the capacity to acknowledge one's faith.

So it is also with events in the world. An adequate causal explanation of them cannot be found by looking to the Church, the Bible, or Jesus

Christ alone. There are natural, economic, social, cultural, political, and other factors involved. But the community of committed believers seeks to interpret and understand the meaning of historical events in the light of its beliefs about God, and man in relation to God. The community of belief acknowledges a common center of meaning in the light of which it views events in the world. Its interpretation of their significance is in some measure determined by an acknowledged loyalty to Jesus Christ. This loyalty is shared, confessed, and in other ways consciously affirmed.

The community of Christian believers, of those who have made a commitment and professed a loyalty, is more restricted in number than the community of Christian language, interpretation, and understanding. Its marks, however, can never be externally measured or precisely determined, for its members often acknowledge their own disloyalty as well as loyalty, unfaith as well as faith. The community of belief cannot be equated with public participation in church services or other activities, for external profession of a covenant is not necessarily correlated with inner trust and belief. Yet this community of belief and commitment exists as a more intensive common identification of Christian people. The Church is a community of belief, commitment, loyalty, trust, faith, and obedience.

The Community of Deed

Belief and commitment are expressed in action. As a community of belief one sees the Church directed toward the primary object of its loyalty, Jesus Christ. As a community of deed ones sees the Church seeking the appropriate expressions of its faith in action. In common action, as in common belief, the unity (or social identity) of the Church is sustained and renewed. Common action in the light of common loyalty brings a new sense of oneness to the members of the Christian community.

The common deeds of Christians are of many kinds, and many of them call attention to the identity of the Church as a distinct human community. Christians may eat together, play together, worship together, engage in deeds of mercy or join in political demonstrations together, or testify to their faith together. Three forms of common action are isolated here for attention as expressions of a common loyalty and faith: worship, evangelical witness, and moral action.

Worship is the common action of Christians as they turn to the source and object of their identity as a people. Its social significance lies in its corporate character, the joining of believers together as they direct their attention toward God. The precise forms of the community of deed in worship differ in various Christian groups. The loud and enthusiastic responses of a Pentecostal congregation to the prayers, Bible reading, hymns, and preaching are very different from the quiet and awesome reverence of a Catholic congregation before the elevation of the Host. The forms of social and psychological interaction are more dramatic and easier to discern in the Pentecostal meeting. The similarities to other emotionally intense and vocal groups are clear, e.g., to a mass political rally or to spectator participation in an exciting athletic event. The Catholic congregation normally does not have so many external forms of common participation in the service as the Pentecostalists do. Yet identity with others, and particularly with other Catholics, is nurtured by the common life of worship at the mass. While the explicit forms of social interaction are not so vocal and observable as in a revival meeting, the meaning of the mass in part suggests to the worshiper his participation in a supratemporal unity, the Body of Christ, to which all true Christians belong.

The types of common deeds in worship differ. Listening to and observing the actions of a priest at an altar, or a preacher in a pulpit, is obviously more passive than singing hymns together, or joining in the recitation of a creed. More intensive and explicit common action on the part of all members of a congregation may stimulate a greater sense of social identity. But other factors also enter in, e.g., the rural or suburban American Protestant congregation may be joined together in bonds of ethnic, cultural, or social values and loyalties. Worship may simply reinforce a sense of common life largely grounded in nonreligious loyalties.[3] Common participation in the actions of worship is intensified as other sources of social loyalty are sustained in the same deeds.

Listening and observing are also common actions. To be sure, members of a more passive congregation, like those of a more active one, bring their dispositions and tacit components of life to the service. This makes for selectivity in hearing, understanding, and evaluating. A Methodist evangelical visiting an Anglo-Catholic mass may find the actions before the altar to be meaningless if not ridiculous. Various Anglicans will see and hear in the light of their own outlooks and needs. But this relativization does not rule out all common elements in listening and observing. A congregation that through years has become

[3] See, e.g., William H. Whyte's chapter "The Church in Suburbia" in *The Organization Man,* New York, 1956, pp. 405-22.

disciplined in its apparently passive participation may be very much united by its worship.

More objective forms of worship, e.g., the celebration of the Mass, as media of common participation are less relative in their personal and cultural components. The actions of Roman Catholic priests are the same in rural and urban parishes, in Bavaria and Brazil, in cathedrals and chapels. The Catholic believer can join in the worship of any congregation or parish. This objectivity in the structure of the acts of common devotion makes possible a social identity that is more universal in scope than that which occurs in more radical Protestant worship life. Particularly in the congregations of nonliturgical, radically democratized American Protestantism, the worship becomes identified with a particular pastor and preacher and his special tastes and convictions. Often one from outside the local congregation feels strange when he attends. American evangelical worship is generally very localized in its social significance, owing in a large measure to the pattern of American churches as voluntary associations. Regardless of its diverse character, however, worship is a form of common action that sustains and renews social identity in churches and the Church.

Common evangelical action is related to worship, though different in the focus of its function. It is directed to those who, in various degrees, are outside of the Christian community. The Church seeks to draw persons into more meaningful relations to the center of its life, Jesus Christ. This is part of its mission or purpose, normatively stated. Socially this implies that the Church seeks to expand its boundaries and to include more persons within the sphere of its life. The definitions of membership, as we have noted, vary. The marks for measuring the expansion vary. Evangelical action, however, is not confined to extending the social boundaries; it is also an effort to bring a more intensive personal identification of every individual with Jesus Christ. Thus there is a double social focus of evangelical action: one directed to those outside the community, and the other to those who already have some identification with it.

Most evangelism is done by the professional clergy. The community has delegated responsibility to its ministers for the recruitment of church members, and for testifying orally and in other ways to the faith of the Church. The communal discipline of evangelism is retained primarily in certain sects, where all members are "soul winners." In the Jehovah's Witnesses, for example, the acceptance of responsibility for evangelism is a basis for membership. In liberal American Protestant churches, e.g., the Methodist Church, institutionalized programs have sought to bring laymen into the work of recruitment and evangelism. In the main, however, evangelism has become a professional task, whether it is directed to the sophisticated university population by such a preacher as Reinhold Niebuhr, or to the masses in Yankee Stadium by Billy Graham, or to a Congo tribe by a missionary.

The lay members of the community, then, often act evangelically only in a secondary way. They are admonished to keep their zeal for this purpose alive. Whether it is for the unsaved heathen of Ecuador, the unchurched residents of a new suburb, or the cultural elite of Greenwich Village, the laity are expected to be concerned for the growth of the Church and for the intensification of participation in its life and meaning. If the commitment to evangelism does not issue in action of person to person, it is carried out in the offerings received for this work in the churches. A common concern for the evangelical mission sustains the social unity of the Church.

A third form of action is the moral witness of the Church in the secular sphere of human life. Churches seek to influence the general moral climate, and particular decisions in society. The Church is a community of moral action. The authority for the moral witness differs from group to group within the Church. For example, the theological foundations vary from the claim of the Roman Catholic Church to a superior knowledge of the natural moral order, to the belief of Holiness groups in the total sanctification of converted believers. The institutional bases differ from the great authority of a papal encyclical and its application by bishops in local political and social situations, to the individual Christian witness to what is right in the light of his private conscience.

The issues addressed are as varied as the bases of authority. Some churches are concerned for the ethics of international relations, especially in light of the power of nuclear weapons; others are concerned for the ethics of young people holding hands in a public park. The precise forms of moral action differ. There are Christian political parties in Western Europe, and there are Christians who are active in secular parties. There are Christians who eschew all party affiliations in the belief that the task of Christian moral action is more spiritual in character, i.e., to convert individual men or to influence a general moral consensus. There are those who confine their action to the amelioration of physical and social suffering.

The Church has always addressed moral issues. The concern for the proper relation of Church and State has existed from New Testament times. Programs for the relief of physical suffering have been continuous through the history of the Church. The Church has addressed the problems of proper family life, usury, just wages and prices, war, and slavery. Special movements in the Church have come to focus around its moral concerns, e.g., the social gospel movement in liberal American Protestantism. Insofar as there has been consensus on moral issues it has often fostered the emergence of new institutions. For example, the American social gospel movement was an important force in the founding of the Federal Council of Churches. A common moral witness brings new experiences of common life and meaning.

The Divisive and Unifying Consequences of Action

Action is a function of commitment and a confirmation of belief. Because the Church believes in Jesus Christ it is committed to him; action, informed and impelled by this commitment and belief, ensues. But the process is neither logically or chronologically in one direction only, i.e., from belief to commitment to action. Christian action may lead to more profound commitment and trust. Common worship is an expression of common belief, but it also nourishes the bonds of trust that it expresses. Evangelism and moral action are expressions of commitment, but in the processes of action the belief and commitment may be intensified, and the meaning of faith and trust clarified.

Like Christian belief, Christian action through worship, evangelism, and moral witness can be socially divisive as well as unifying. Special communities of Christians form around particular patterns of common deeds. These may be coextensive with existing denominational groups, or they may cross old lines and draw members from various churches.

The divisive significance of worship is reflected in the place of importance this subject holds in ecumenical discussion. Worship "after the manner of Friends" is sharply different from Catholic or Lutheran worship. The revivalist tradition has its established modes for renewing men's consciousness of God. Various traditions converge; an eclecticism appears which removes some traditional marks of division. Many Midwestern Quaker congregations have preachers who prepare sermons and an "order of service." Methodists have reassessed their separation from the Church of England's Book of Common Prayer, and sought to revive some of its elements. Presbyterians and Congregationalists look back to Geneva for a pattern of liturgical life that is theologically viable. There are movements toward establishing common forms; most American Lutheran denominations now use a common service and hymnal. Concurrently, however, new sects emerge that eschew the traditional patterns.

In evangelism as well, there are separations by denominational lines, and groups that agree across these traditional barriers. American Southern Baptists have generally approved of Billy Graham's missions, but Presbyterians are divided in their opinion. The local supporters of a Graham campaign may include Episcopalians, Methodists, Presbyterians, Lutherans, and Baptists. The social complexion would be different, however, if the "faith healer" Oral Roberts were to seek a supporting committee, or if the lay visitation evangelism program of the Methodist Church were to be used. In the work of missions to non-Christian cultures the divisions over proper evangelical methods are equally sharp. The loyalties to various ways of work divide the missionaries of some denominations, and form new groups across traditional lines.

The same processes occur with reference to moral action. The strife within Protestant denominations in the United States during 1945-1955 illustrates this. The validity of work engaged in for decades by denominational agencies was challenged, as for example in the Congregational Christian Churches. New institutions and social groups emerged around various definitions of the nature and purpose of the moral witness of the Church. In the United States a small group called Christian Action formed around the inspiration of the person and action of Reinhold Niebuhr. Concurrently, politically conservative movements, e.g., Spiritual Mobilization, gained strength. New social patterns of loyalty emerged around various points of consensus about the proper bases and methods of Christian moral action.

Patterns of Church action are both divisive and unifying. The basic purposes of action can be defined and supported widely, though the particular forms of action are often the causes of division. Whether in large groups of Christians or small, however, the common deeds sustain the common loyalty and social identity of churches and the Church.

Men join many associations and organizations. They are loyal to various groups, and to the principles for which they stand. The act of joining, or of giving assent to membership, gives precise definition to the boundaries of various groups, including the Church. Action in behalf of principles to which a group is loyal sustains identification with it, whether it be the nation-state or the Boy Scouts.

The Church is the community that is loyal to Jesus Christ, its unique source of meaning. Christians self-consciously seek in him, and in the life of the Church, the basis for their lives. They commit themselves to the Church, and to God toward whom the Church points. This commitment is one of faith and trust; Christians not only have knowledge of their center of loyalty, but they believe in him, and rest their lives in him. The religious dimensions of faith, trust, belief, and obedience may or may not be different in quality from the loyalties men have to other groups. The principal difference is in the object of faith and obedience. Faith and trust in God is acknowledged and confessed; it impels and informs action. The Church is a community of belief and action.

CHAPTER 8

Social and Theological
Interpretation of the Church

In the preceding chapters the Church has been interpreted within a framework of social thought. This has not required the exclusion of theology, but where it was introduced the interest has been in its *function* in the historical community of Christians. The Church cannot be understood socially without studying its system of beliefs, for its particularity is defined by its beliefs. We have shown that various human social processes in the life of the Christian community are not unique to it, but rather are common to a variety of human communities. In a social interpretation, then, the continuity and social identity of the Christian society can be seen as part of the general social and historical life of man. Even the elements of faith, commitment, and belief have their approximate counterparts in other groups.

In one sense the preceding chapters are a deliberate effort at reductionism; we have tried insofar as possible to account for the life of the Church as an historical community without primary reference to ideas that are part of the disciplines of Christian doctrine and Biblical studies. Such concepts have been introduced only to show their social function.

The human studies have provided a framework in which to interpret not only the aspects of the life of the Church that it shares with all communities, but also its particularities and differentia. We have deliberately been as inclusive as possible in the social interpretation of the Church. In part this implies a critique of the theological reductionism that is characteristic of much of the contemporary interpretation of the Church, especially by professional theologians. By theological reductionism we mean the exclusive use of Biblical and doctrinal language in the interpretation of the Church. Many make the explicit or tacit assumption that the Church is so absolutely unique in character that it can be understood only in its own private language. We have shown how the life of the Church can be understood in the language of social thought. Therefore questions arise. How can the same phenomenon, the Church, be understood from two radically diverse perspectives? Does the use of doctrinal language require inherently the exclusion of the language of social thought? Does a social interpretation of the Church necessarily exclude the more distinctively theological and doctrinal interpretation? If the two are not mutually exclusive, how can the significance of the social processes and elements be theologically understood? Since the center of our interpretation is social, the last question is most important for us.

Institution and Fellowship (Koinonia):[1] *social and theological understanding*

The problem we have defined can be developed with reference to a particular aspect of the Church's life, namely, its existence as both a fellowship and an institution. The existence of both elements can be understood as social necessities on the one hand, or as God's ordering and gift on the other. The persisting institutional patterns of ministry, sacraments, and other forms of Church life are from a social point of view necessary developments in order to preserve the historical existence of the community, and particularly its special identity as a Christian community. From a theological point of view they can be under-

---

[1] Here "fellowship" is introduced to refer to a special aspect of community, namely, the interpersonal, subjective sense of oneness that exists among Christians. Its chief merit is that it avoids using "community" again in a special sense. Its dangers are manifold, especially in the United States, where the word is used to mean everything from a teen-age club to the special characteristics of spiritual and psychological intimacy in the churches' use of group dynamics techniques. The word "communion" is preferable, but lends itself to confusion with the sacrament.

stood as God's order for the Church. They have been instituted by God for the existence of his people; they are grounded in the New Testament account of what God has done for man. The fellowship of Christians in one spirit and mind can be understood in a double way as well. Socially it can be seen as a unity of common memory, loyalty, and meanings that are kept alive through the common life of the Church. Christians are united in the inner life of their common faith and commitment as well as by participation in the same institutions. Theologically this spiritual unity is interpreted as a gift of God in Jesus Christ. It is the unity of the Body of which Christ is the head; it is the mark of the work of the Holy Spirit of God among his people.[2]

The Church is both a fellowship and an institution. These two aspects of its life are necessary to each other and to the whole for the continuation of the Church and its social unity. We have seen how the objective expressions of the meanings of the Church (its institutional forms) are necessary to preserve the less institutionalized forms of common life and spirit. Its political structures, the Bible, the ministry, the sacraments, all make possible processes of life in which persons become identified with Jesus Christ, and with the common life of those who believe in him. The Bible is the most important objectification of the meaning of Jesus Christ and life in relation to him. Indeed, both the Old and New Testaments are expressions of the common life of a people who understand themselves and all events of history to be related to God. The Bible in its various types of literature carries in a relatively stable form the meanings that mark the Christian community in distinction from other human groups. It bears the possibility of those meanings becoming the center of life for individual persons, and remaining the center of life for the whole Church. It is not sufficient in and of itself, however, and therefore other institutional forms are necessary. The communication and interpretation of its meaning depend upon the existence of certain offices and rites. The ministry exists in part to make living and internal the meanings carried externally and objectively in the Bible. The Lord's Supper is a rite in which the significance of the death of Jesus Christ is remembered again. Liturgies as a whole carry out for each congregation and generation a pattern of meaning in which men can participate.

[2] My reflections on the particular question of institution and *koinonia* have been informed by both sociological and theological literature. Recently they have come to focus in discussions in the Faith and Order Commission on Institutionalism of the World Council of Churches.

These institutional forms are essential for the continuation and re-creation of a more subjective, internal, and interpersonal common life. The Church consists not only of these structures, but of a common inner life and spirit as well. But the continuation of the common inner life and spirit requires the guidance, informing power, and judgment of the objectified institutional forms. The importance of both institution and fellowship can be seen historically in the Reformation. Both Luther and Calvin, in their writings on the Church, defined the proper order and life of the Church on the one hand against the spiritualist sectarians, and on the other hand against the Catholics.

The sectarians on the left-wing fell into the error of assuming the rightness of the community's understanding and action because they were presumably informed directly by the Bible, Jesus Christ, or the Holy Spirit. The clergy and other forms lost their traditional functions. Belief in the immediacy of the presence of the Spirit led to bizarre interpretations of the Gospel, and to strange moral actions among some groups. Both belief and action were not brought properly under the criticism and judgment of the objectifications (especially clergy, liturgy, and creeds) that historically kept the community's identity as Church. Without being informed and guided by these institutional forms the free spirit could lead to practices and beliefs not identifiable with the Christian tradition.[3] In a similar way the New England Puritans, in their actions of religious intolerance against Anne Hutchinson and Roger Williams, feared the consequences of religious inner certainty that was not guided by the traditional objective institutions. Ignoring the issue of religious toleration, one can see in these examples the belief that the common inner life of the Christian community must be informed, judged, and guided by its institutional patterns. The identity of the inner life as Christian depends upon the proper functioning of the institutional forms. One cannot conceive of the continuation of the communal, inner aspects of Christian church life without proper external institutional forms.[4]

[3] This illustration is too brief to do justice to more than the general point, i.e., that the Reformers were suspicious of those who viewed the Church as a "fellowship," in the radical sense, to the ignoring of institutional forms. All groups, interestingly, claimed Biblical authority.

[4] An issue implied here is the determination of what institutional forms and objective expressions are the *sine qua non* of the Church. The so-called "non-Church movement" in Japan seeks to live and survive only on the basis of the Bible and its informal exposition in the community. From Anglican, Lutheran, and Catholic points of view this group is properly called "non-Church," though

The Reformers' arguments against the Catholics illustrate the other side of the social nature of the Church. The institutional forms in and of themselves do not necessarily create the inner community of faith and belief; indeed, they are subject to severe perversion. Institutionalization or objectification can proceed to such a point that men begin to identify the existence of the Church with the existence of objects: the Bible, sacramental practice, and priesthood. The Reformation is a social testimony to the inadequacy of excessive objectification and institutionalization. The forms had both to express and inform the subjective inner life of the Church. The Church exists only where the meanings objectively carried by the forms are subjectively appropriated and believed in by persons. The inner community has a quality of common spirit as these forms provide the center of meaning and faith for personal life and for the common life of Christians. The continuing protest of new sectarian groups since the Reformation, like those before it, testifies to the felt need of this interpersonal unity of meaning, subjectively appropriated and believed. Most of the historical protests have been against excessive objectification and institutionalization, and have sought to revive the spiritual fellowship that seems to have existed among the early Christians, and which many Christians continue to believe in as both reality and goal. Institutional forms are more meaningful and presumed to be more authentic when they express the living spirit of the Church. There can be a sense of personal participation in the reading of the Scripture, the preached word, and the sacraments. Creeds are confessions of the personal faith of individuals and the common faith of the Church.[5]

Institution and fellowship are necessary to each other. The Church consists of both, and its identity depends upon the continuation of

the group believes itself to be part of the Christian community. For Anglicans, by contrast, the *sine qua non* for proper order includes Bible, ecumenical creeds, the sacraments, and a rightly ordered ministry. From a social standpoint one would predict that the non-Church movement will develop institutional patterns by which both its particular identity as a group and its identity with the Church as a whole will be sustained. For a brief description of the Japanese movement, see Emil Brunner, "A Unique Christian Mission: The Mukyokai ("Non-Church") Movement in Japan," in W. Leibrecht (ed.), *Religion and Culture,* pp. 287-90.

[5] Two other problems often exist in institutionalization. (1) Institutional forms, particularly offices in the Church, provide the occasion for concentration of power, corrupt coercion of others, and pride for the office holder. (2) Some forms also lose any significant function and become vestigial, i.e., they are maintained with no more meaning than that they are traditional.

both. This social explanation, however, is unsatisfactory to both theologians and devout laymen. They hold that God has given man the Church. Its being is a mark of the presence and activity of God through Christ and the Holy Spirit. Its order is ordained or instituted by God. The Bible is not only an expression of lived experience and meaning; it is the gospel of God, the news of God's mighty acts of creation, preservation, and redemption. The sacraments are not only rites that have emerged to carry the community's memory from one generation to another, or to initiate one into the Church. They are given by God, ordained by Jesus Christ his Son as means by which God restores and renews faith in the lives of persons and of the whole Church. The ministry is not only a social necessity comparable to the need for leadership and representative human symbols in other communities. It represents an order of life in which God has called and ordained some to special functions as expressions of his care and good pleasure for his people.

And certainly Jesus Christ is not only a center of meaning, or a collective representation that gives unity and continuity to a historical society. He is the revelation of God; in him believers know God's mercy and wrath, God's grace and judgment. Indeed, some plainly say "Jesus Christ is God." He is the Savior. He is God in the form of a servant, God humbling himself in the form of man. Nor is Jesus Christ only a person and event to be remembered; he is living. The Church is his Body in which he dwells; he continues to provide grace and truth to his people, and to judge and redeem them.

The common inner life of the Church is not only the effect of processes of internalization of objectified meaning. It is not only the subjective counterpart to the objective signs and marks of life given in institutional forms. It is *koinonia,* a fellowship given by Jesus Christ and sustained by the activity of the Holy Spirit of God. It is a gift, and not just a natural outcome of a social process. God himself is present among men, and makes himself and his actions known in the common life of the Church. The unity and power of the Church are gifts of God's love, and marks of his living presence in the Church.

Thus we Christians do not come to a satisfactory self-understanding, of our common life unless we see it in relation to God's purpose and action, past, present, and anticipated. An exclusively social interpretation is a reductionism to Christian believers. We confess that the Church is instituted by God, created, sustained, and redeemed by his self-revelation and activity among us. Our fellowship is a manifestation of God's holy love dwelling in and among us. Institution and fellowship are to be understood not only as the effects of social processes, but also as the gift and work of God. To make this confession, however, is not to deny the reality of the processes and patterns analyzed in preceeding chapters.[6]

Limitations of Reductionisms: doctrinal and social

Both doctrinal and social reductionism must be avoided in an understanding of the Church. A doctrinal reductionism refuses to take seriously the human elements in the Church's life, or if it acknowledges them it does not explore or explicate them except in doctrinal language. The definition of the Church may focus on what is considered to be the essence of the Church; this may be defined in such a way as to exclude the social functions and structures that the Church shares with all societies. As indicated in the first chapter, the reader occasionally has difficulty in knowing whether some theologians are referring to anything historical and social in character in their treatises on the Church. If they refer to the historical community it is not easy to understand the relation between the essence and the historical processes we have delineated. Many theologians ignore part of their task in ecclesiology, i.e., to make theologically intelligible the human forms and processes that can be understood and interpreted from a social perspective.[7]

Since the starting point and focus of attention of the present book is a social interpretation of the Church, the limitations of a social reductionism are a larger issue for us. In the preceding chapters an opera-

[6] To elaborate this bi-polar view and its implications for church life is a temptation, but the task is not precisely germane to the purpose of this essay. Nevertheless, one is provoked to ask Troeltsch's question, "What is the best institutional form of church life for the modern world?" As between the antitheses of orthodoxy and heresy, which risk would one choose? Are the dangers of "objectivism" more treacherous in our time than the dangers of "subjectivism"? Has the notion of *koinonia* become too identified with the interpersonal coziness of confession sharing in "Christian cells," or with the social congeniality of an American rural or suburban church? Does Christian fellowship imply personal relations? What kind? Men's clubs in which loyalty to a particular political party is reinforced by "fellowship" in the Church? Or have we gone too far in the other direction? Is right belief now too much ascendant as the mark of the Church? Right order? Do we worry too much about the "ecclesiastical validity" of everything from the college chaplaincy to the every-member canvass? About the "authority" for every act and office? Are we binding the Holy Spirit to overvalued human forms?

The point of view of this essay does not permit categorical answers to these questions. For example, a Church of Sweden parish is called a "congregation," but it is really an objective, Word of God dispensary for those who want to come

tional limitation has been imposed on the interpretation. The Church has been interpreted within a closed circle around man, history, society, and man's beliefs. The reality to be considered for interpretation and analysis is thus limited. For most social scientists and many social philosophers such a limitation of reality is correct. They are committed to the view that there is no reality beyond what can be understood by the "empirical" disciplines, or can be perceived and observed through the senses. Our intention has not been to make a dogma of such a position. Rather we have interpreted the Church within terms of the natural in order to indicate certain aspects of Church life that can be illumined perhaps best from such a perspective.

A theological approach relates the life of the Church primarily to God; a social interpretation defines the processes and patterns with primary reference to their social function. The difference between them lies in *the understanding of that to which Church life is related,* or from which it has its source. In our interpretation of the function of Scripture, for example, we pointed to its use in relation to individual persons, to the Church as a community, and to particular church groups. We indicated how it provides a center of meaning for the integration of personal life, and how this center can be held in common by many people. Thus the social unity and continuity of the Church is abetted by the existence of the Bible. Indeed, the Bible is one of the conditions out of which the community grows and continues. Such an interpretation of the function of the Bible is important. By looking at it

---

and receive a bit of law and gospel. Most Swedish parishes are devoid of every trait of interpersonal relations an American, even in the Episcopal tradition (which is currently infatuated with group-dynamics), would expect to find in a congregation. One answer is required in the Church of Sweden. But another is required where "our kind of people" working together in a great deal of social interaction in women's circles, church committees, youth groups, etc., is confused with the Church whose Head and Ruler is Jesus Christ.

Or, one worries about theological students who say that a communion service is not "valid" because there was no oral general confession (though penitential Psalms were read). This is "playing church," and is potentially a serious problem. But one also worries about a casual Lord's Supper in which the words of institution are left out and there is no prayer of thanksgiving.

All this implies not indecision but decisiveness about particular questions in particular places. More generally, however, it implies confidence that God uses many particular historical and social forms for his work in the Church and the world.¹ The adaptive human community, always governed by loyalty to God in Christ, always asking what Christ's lordship requires and permits in this place or at this time, is an instrument of God's action. One can have confidence in adaptivity as long as the objectifications of Jesus Christ, in Bible, creeds, etc., continue to have authority for the Church. They check bizarre theologies and patterns of church

primarily in the light of its social significance for the Church one may see aspects of its use that would be hidden from an interpretation that began with the doctrine of Scripture as a medium of God's revelation. Precisely the positive value of a social reductionism is its greatest weakness for the theologian and Christian believer. The Bible is not only a holy book that sustains a continuing community as its members become identified as Christians through its study and proclamation. For Christians, the Bible is a medium of revelation; it not only tells the community about itself but about God. Its function must be seen not only within the circle around men, history, society, and beliefs, but also in relation to God and his disclosure of himself in his actions.

The Church, like the community of Old Testament times, comes to a more inclusive self-understanding when it looks at itself in relation to God or looks at God in relation to itself. We have interpreted the Church only in the light of the function of its *beliefs about* God, that is, from the manward side. When the importance of faith was introduced it was limited to the human side, whereas the Church generally understands faith to be a gift of God's grace. When the idea of covenant was introduced, we did not deal with the Church's affirmation that God has initiated the covenant, and that the human community exists through prior divine purpose and action. The Holy Communion not only keeps the memory of past events and the whole community alive, but is a means by which God's grace is given to man. The Christian understanding of the Church, then, breaks through the circle imposed by an exclusively social interpretation. It views human experience in the Church in the light of God's revelation and activity. The human agencies and processes whose function can be socially understood are mirrors in which God's presence is made known to man. They are God's creation, and a means of his redeeming work.

---

life. Thus one returns to the bi-polar character of the Church—an inner fellowship informed by relatively stable objective signs.

[7] Chap. 1 cited several theological treatises on the nature of the Church that come to some resolution of this issue. Other writers have also come to grips with it. Professor John Knox, e.g., in *Criticism and Faith,* New York, 1952, pp. 29-30, comes close to identifying the revelation with the community. C. C. Morrison, in *What is Christianity?,* Chicago, 1940, makes no serious effort to distinguish the two; Christianity is virtually the Church and its history; see especially pp. 66-69. H. N. Wieman, in *The Source of Human Good,* Chicago, 1947, pp. 39 ff., describes the community-creating event and process in such a way that God is virtually identified with this process.

The Unfinished Task

Two aspects of theological analysis are involved in breaking the circle around the human and cultural. In introducing them some of the major issues in the interpretation of God's relation to the world are opened, and they cannot be discussed at length here. One is the problem of how to understand the *divine causality and governance* of processes that can be interpreted in terms of human and natural life, i.e., can be interpreted as if God did not exist. The other problem, not unrelated, is the *religious meaning and significance* of what can be interpreted as natural structures and processes. The first problem is the manner of God's relation to social processes in terms of his nature as the ground of their being, their final cause, or their indwelling power and life. The second problem is the meaning of these processes in the light of the Church's confession of God known in Jesus Christ.

The implications of both problems involve the whole realm of theological discussion. Here we can only suggest the manner in which theological and social interpretations of the Church might be brought together. The issue of the causal relation of God to social processes leads to problems of philosophical theology, whether this discipline is pursued in the language of the philosophers (e.g., being and becoming), or whether it is a philosophical discussion thinly disguised in the language of the Bible and Christian doctrine (e.g., God ordering the world through his law). The issue of the meaning of life in the Church under the lordship of Jesus Christ leads to many problems of Biblical interpretation, "confessional" theology, and particular doctrines. Both would require clarification of the theological method used.

The two issues of causal analysis and of meaning in relation to God can be brought together, however, by the now popular truism "God acts in history." From this statement an important implication can be drawn for our problem. The affirmation that God acts in history means that in his power and good pleasure he chooses to use that which can be interpreted without reference to him as a means of ruling and making himself known. He uses the realm of the natural and the social as an agency or a mask for his presence and will toward men. The issue of causal relation is taken care of in the highly ambiguous language of God *acting in* history. The questions a metaphysician would raise about the relation of the abiding, eternal, and simple unity to the changing, temporal, and complex multiplicity have been answered in various ways to the satisfaction of various theologians, e.g., in the language of Plato, Aquinas, Tillich, Whitehead, or F. R. Tennant. Or they can be left unanswered by the now commonplace assertion that is sometimes a profound excuse for the lack of intellectual clarity and rigor, namely, that it is a "statement of faith," or a "faith assertion." Christians assert in faith that God has made known his capacity to perform his mighty and his commonplace deeds in the realm of the contingent, the human, and the transitory.

Thus the issue of cause is brought together with the issue of meaning. The cause provides the meaning; the meaning points to the cause. The meaning of the social processes can be understood in the light of God's disclosure of himself in Jesus Christ, in the Biblical testimony to God's deeds of creation and renewal in the old and new covenants, and in the light of the theological implications of this revelation. God uses human needs, for example, as a medium through which he gathers his people together, and through which his divine ministry becomes a ministry among men. Thus the commonplace, e.g., the American rural Protestant church supper, can be a human gathering and occasion through which God can act and speak. The patterns of political life in the churches can be the awesomely human social instruments through which God orders the common life of his people. They are the necessary instruments for the expression of this will and work in a given historical context. They are also the occasion for human pride and sin to take specific shape. The internalization processes are the human counterparts to the prior action of God's power and spirit, bringing men to a knowledge of Jesus Christ through the Church. Indeed, they may be the marks of the work of the Holy Spirit. The elements of faith and commitment are the human subjective counterparts to the divine initiative of grace. God initiates the covenant; God initiates personal faith. The actions characteristic of the Christian community are means of God's action, disclosing himself in worship, drawing men to himself in evangelism, and exercising his sovereignty in the world through the moral actions of men.

The Bible testifies to this use of the human and the historical by God. God created men. The prophets wrote of Assyria as the rod of God's anger against his chosen people, and they proclaim his power to use a "broken reed," an unfaithful human servant. St. Paul says that we have our treasure in earthen vessels, that there is nothing in which we can glory, but that God empowers man to do his will. The Incarnation is a testimony to the power of God to use the human as a means of his disclosure and action. God empties himself, takes the form of a servant, and so reveals himself to men. In the light of the knowledge of God in faith we can understand the meaning of the human, social processes in relation to God, the one who transcends the limitations of the circle around man, society, and beliefs.

Such an interpretation has a religious persuasiveness in spite of its ambiguities. It does not set the eternal over against the temporal, the abiding against the changing, the simple unity against the complex multiplicity. Rather it asserts that the one who is above history enters into history, and the eternal one is present in time. A social interpretation of the Church need not lead to religious uncertainty and despair. Christians can accept the human, social, and historical not merely in resignation to fate, but in the confidence that this realm is of significance to God and his activity. The problem of the believer, then, is not how to reconcile the social and historical character of the Church with a suprahistorical or even historical essence. This problem is avoided by not admitting its premise, namely, that a suprahistorical or essential nature of the Church is more real, purer, or of greater value than its changing social character. The issue is no longer the eternal absolute against the temporal relativity. Rather, Christians can affirm the historical community and participate in it in a clear and certain knowledge that its humanness is in the power of God. Precisely the natural community, the political community, the community of language, interpretation and understanding, the community of belief and action, is the Church, God's people. The human processes of its common life are means of God's ordering, sustaining, and redeeming his people.[8]

[8] Karl Barth develops one theological basis on which man's temporality and contingency can be accepted in his discussion of time. His view has implications for our discussion of the Church. Like all past, present, and future, the Church's past is God's past, its present God's present, and its future God's future. God is in time and the Lord of time. Man in faith is assured that this is so. The Lord of time is the gracious God revealed in Jesus Christ. This knowledge frees us from enslavement to timeful existence, and permits us to live in it as we are called to do so.

God has no past that does not contain his present and future, no present that does not contain his past and future, and no future that does not contain his past and present. In contrast, according to Barth, our human experience of time is a succession of past, present, and future in which our present is only as our past ceases to be, and our future only as it becomes our present. In Jesus Christ, however, we know that God has established his lordship over temporality. Thus God's time gives meaning to our time, and our time to God's time.

In consequence of this we need not be preoccupied with the past, seeking to reconstruct it and to find in it laws for life. This preoccupation with the past is uncreative and reactionary. Nor do we need to become anxious to forget our past by living for the future; this is impossible because we cannot leave our past com-

The affirmation of the Church as an historical society does not imply its divinization, or an assumption of its inerrancy, moral rectitude, or spiritual purity in any sectarian or Catholic fashion. A social interpretation exposes the elements of humanity in the Church; i.e., its contingency, historical relativity, and dependence on universal social processes. This is no counsel of despair, however. Indeed, it is a counsel of strength and hope, for it is precisely the human community that God has called, and through which he acts. Its human social character is essential to its purpose. The Church is not so identified with the being of God himself that it becomes virtually an object of adoration, or a fourth member of the Godhead. Rather, its power and effectiveness depend upon its humanity, even its sinful humanity.

Because it is a *human community* the Church can make Christ present to men. Its social adaptiveness is a strength rather than a weakness, a good rather than an evil. It must find the political forms, patterns of interpretation, and liturgies through which Christ can make himself present to the disinherited Negroes and Puerto Ricans of Manhattan, the Hindu Tamils of Ceylon, the dying aristocracy of Western Europe, and the people of Eastern Europe under Soviet domination. Failure to adapt means failure in its mission. It found patterns effective for its mission among the serfs of medieval Christendom and the *bourgeoisie* of the mercantile age; it must find them for the rising nationalists of Africa and Asia in our century. It has defined its beliefs in relation to Platonism through Augustine and the Church Fathers, to Aristotelianism through St. Thomas, to existentialism through Bultmann; it must define them in relation to logical analysis through theologians of our decade. The Church's continuity, unity, and fulfillment of purpose require social processes.[9]

---

pletely behind. In faith in God, and in knowledge of the abiding character of God's time, we can learn from the past without putting faith in the past.

By implication, the Church's history can be its informer without being its tyrant. Both preoccupation with the past and anxious effort to forget the past are foreclosed, for the Church's past is in God. It is under his judgment and therefore it cannot be ignored; it is in his mercy and therefore need not be feared. So also the future is in God. It is neither the object of anxious preoccupation nor is it to be ignored. It is God's future, a filled future. The Church can be free from fear of the future, and yet act responsibly in and toward it.

Kirchliche Dogmatik, II, 1, Zurich, 1940, pp. 689 ff., contains the discussion of the timefulness of God; III, 2, Zurich, 1948, pp. 638 ff., contains the discussion of the consequences of faith for understanding our past; pp. 659 ff. for understanding the future.

[9] This theological interpretation of the social character of the Church is unfinished; our intention here is only to indicate directions it might take. In a

The Church is a chameleon.[10] It finds colors that fit it into various environments. It continues, yet changes; this is the value of its social nature. Yet it stands always under the order and judgment of God to whom it professes loyalty and in whom it believes. It is a human community, with a particular vocation, purpose, and power.

To the Jews I became as a Jew, in order to win Jews; to those under the law I became as one under the law—though not being myself under the law—that I might win those under the law. To those outside the law I became as one outside the law—not being without law toward God but under the law of Christ—that I might win those outside the law. To the weak I became weak, that I might win the weak. I have become all things to all men, that I might by all means save some. I do it all for the sake of the gospel. . . .

But we have this treasure in earthen vessels, to show that the transcendent power belongs to God and not to us.[11]

---

further development of it, one would do well to form his convictions in relation to four discussions that bear on the issues involved: Schleiermacher, *The Christian Faith*, Edinburgh, 1928, pp. 532-695; Bonhoeffer, *Sanctorum Communio*; Karl Barth, *Church Dogmatics*, IV, 2, Edinburgh, 1958, pp. 614-726; and Claude Welch, *The Reality of the Church*.

[10] The phrase was suggested to me by Dr. Hans Dumbois of Heidelberg, in a discussion.

[11] St. Paul, in I Cor. 9:20-23, and II Cor. 4:7, RSV.

Time and Community:
A Discussion

Chapters 4, 5, and 6 are based upon an interpretation of the relation between time and community. The treatment of this problem by various philosophers is worthy of more attention than it received in the text. The question can be set as follows: What is the importance of its existence through time for the inner life of a community? This question can be divided into two. First, how does the historical timeful character of a social group enter into its subjective unity, or its unity of meaning? Second, how can the subjective unity of meaning in a community be maintained through time and history?

In order to answer these questions it is necessary to ask further questions. Since the inner unity of a community is in large part a unity of meanings shared by persons, how do the dimensions of temporality and historicity enter into the self? The significance of temporality for the community can be approached through an understanding of its significance for selfhood. Then the next question becomes: How can different persons have memories and expectations in common? In answering this we are involved in the second principal question stated above, i.e., how community continues through time, for the same aspects of experience are involved in both. It is through the existence of common expressions or signs of the inner life of a community of the past that, on the one hand, the past can enter into the subjective experience of the present, and on the other hand, the subjective unity can persist through time.

To explore these issues further it is instructive to examine some theories of time that are relevant to understanding the nature of self and community. In recent discussions a distinction has been made between the "Christian view of time" and the "Greek view of time." Robert E. Cushman identifies Augustine's view of temporal duration in relation to the self as the Christian view of time. The Greek view measures time in relation to nature, and understands eternity to be absolute timelessness.[1] Within Cushman's distinction, we are primarily concerned with the Christian view of time. Erich Frank calls the concept of the absolute timelessness of existence the Chris-

[1] Cushman, "Greek and Christian Views of Time," *Journal of Religion*, Vol. 33 (1953), pp. 254-65.

tian view of eternity. The Greek view of eternity he calls "everness" of a
"perpetual present" (this is his translation of *aeon*).[2] Tillich says that "eternity is neither timelessness nor the endlessness of time"; rather the Greek
aiones means the power of embracing all periods of time.[3] One concern is
not so much with the idea of eternity, as it is with time in relation to persons
and history. Therefore discussion is limited to contributions relevant to the
issues of temporality and selfhood, and temporality and community.

The Self and Time

Interpretations of the self and time tend to center around two poles. One
type of discussion conceives of the essential self as ultimately transcending
temporality; the other understands the self to be deeply conditioned by its
temporal existence. These two tendencies of thought have distinct consequences for the interpretation of community and time. The former mini-
mizes the extent of interpenetration of selves that is involved in community
and tends to relate persons to one another through an external normative
obligation. The latter is more organic in character; there is a real involvement of selves in one another. Immanuel Kant and Søren Kierkegaard represent the former understanding of the self and community; Augustine and
all those who have affinities with his discussion of time represent the latter
type. Henri Bergson, Josiah Royce, Wilhelm Dilthey, and G. H. Mead are
all to some extent within the Augustinian tradition on the issue of time and
the self. Bergson and Royce have metaphysical doctrines within which they
account for duration and temporality as they are known in human experience. Dilthey and Mead eschew discussion of the metaphysical consequences
of their theories of history, the self, and time.[4]

Kant and Kierkegaard offer one alternative for dealing with time and the
self. Discussion of Kant's view of time is usually based on the *Critique of
Pure Reason*. There the most concise definition one finds of time in relation
to the self is that time is "a pure form of sensible intuition."[5] The question
that is usually asked of Kant's theory of time, however, can be reversed.

[2] Frank, *Philosophical Understanding and Religious Truth*, New York, 1945,
pp. 60, 76-77. Both Frank and Cushman note that Aristotle gives a hint of the
possibility of measuring time not only against nature, but also against the self.
See Aristotle, *Physics*, iv, 10, 1-2.

[3] Paul Tillich, *Systematic Theology*, I, Chicago, 1951, p. 274.

[4] Only insofar as they are relevant to the present problem will the metaphysics
of these men be considered.

[5] I. Kant, *Critique of Pure Reason*, trans. N. K. Smith, London, 1953, p. 75.
Erich Frank answers the question of the locus of time with "there is only one,
acceptable answer, that given by Augustine and repeated by Kant, it is in our
soul. . . ." Frank, *op. cit.*, p. 65. Frank oversimplifies the two theories. Time is in
the soul for Augustine and Kant alike in only a minimal sense. Insofar as it is
a passive form of sensible intuition for Kant it is far from Augustine's analysis of
time in relation to the self. The factor of expectation, however, is involved in
Kant's theory of the moral self. Augustine's theory is discussed below.

First one can ask, what is the self? and then, what is time for and in the self? In approaching it this way our attention is brought to the *Critique of Practical Reason* and other ethical writings. If one begins with the existing, acting moral self, rather than with the knowing mind and the external world, one would suspect that a more dynamic view of time in relation to the self might be found.

For Kant, however, man as a being in himself transcends natural or rational time. The freedom of man in its essence is freedom from temporality; the moral self is not determined by its historical existence. He wrote, "Actually, if the actions of man, as they pertain to his determinations in time, were not merely properties of his being as appearance but also of his being as a thing in himself, freedom could not be saved."[6] The possibility of the moral, free self is predicated upon Kant's distinction between the sensuous and the intelligible modes of presentation, the sensuous and the noumenal aspects of the self. Temporal and historical determination are involved in the self at the level of consequences of actions and decisions; these are in the realm of the sensuous. In this realm there is determination, and determination involves temporal succession. But the noumenal self is free from temporal and historical determination, though it looks forward to the coming kingdom of ends. The creation of the self at the noumenal level is the creation of the thing-in-itself, the creation of autonomy and perfect freedom. The noumenal self transcends natural and rational time.[7] The essential self, once created, is independent even of the Creator; there is no determination of the self but its own determination.

This means, then, that the noumenal self is not significantly conditioned

[6] Kant, *Critique of Practical Reason and Other Writings in Moral Philosophy,* trans. and ed. Lewis W. Beck, Chicago, 1949, p. 206. To see time and space as attributes of things in themselves is to be forced to admit "fatalism of actions," or else to fall into a contradiction.

[7] Cf. *ibid.,* pp. 207-8, "If existence in time is merely a sensuous mode of presentation belonging to thinking beings in the world, and consequently does not concern the things-in-themselves, the creation of these beings is a creation of things-in-themselves, because the concept of creation does not belong to the sensuous mode of conceiving of existence or to causality but can be referred only to noumena. Consequently, if I say of beings in the world of sense that they are created, I regard them only as noumena. . . . Now, assuming existence in time to hold only of appearances and not of things-in-themselves, if it is possible to affirm freedom without detriment to the natural mechanism of actions as appearances, then the circumstances that the acting beings are creatures cannot make the least difference in the argument, because creation concerns their intelligible but not their sensuous existence, and therefore creation cannot be regarded as the determining ground of appearances. It would turn out very differently if the beings in the world existed as things-in-themselves in time, since the Creator of substance would then be also the author of the entire mechanism of this substance." Cf. H. J. Paton, *The Categorical Imperative,* London, 1948, pp. 234 f., 253 f. Paton stresses that in Kant's theory we have two aspects of the self, and not two independent selves.

by history and community. The self can choose community, as in its adherence to a social realm of ends, but the choice itself is made out of radical freedom. The self is not only free from determination by history and community, but its freedom appears to separate it from the sustaining power of history and community. The actions of the free self have temporal and historical consequences determined by the ordering of nature. But the sharp distinction remains between the free self, transcending historical and temporal determination, and the consequences of the decisions of the self that are part of the order of natural time and determination. The relationship between the moral self and the realm of historical and natural causality is by and large unilateral.

Kant arrived at this view of the self and its radical freedom by a process of analytical argument. He tried to account for the moral experience of man. This could not be accounted for to his satisfaction within an order of natural determination, and consequently he found that the practical reason required the postulate of radical freedom in order to account for the moral life. Whether this postulate adequately illumines the unity of the self, however, is an open question. The self that makes free moral decisions is acting within community and history. Are its decisions exempt from the conditioning of the particular history and community in which it exists? Does not its involvement in the order of sensible determination enter into its moral decisions?[8]

Søren Kierkegaard's understanding of the self in relation to time (and to community) is essentially Kantian. In positing the possibility of the Christian's absolute contemporaneity with Christ, Kierkegaard asserts that the self has a relation to the Eternal that has consequences in time. Christ is the absolute; the relation of the individual to Christ is one of inwardness—subjective truth—which is not temporally and historically conditioned. The real history of Christianity is the history of individuals who have an inward relation to the eternally contemporaneous Christ, "For what true Christians there are in each generation are contemporary with Christ, have nothing to do with Christians of former generations, but everything to do with the contemporary Christ."[9] The history of Christianity would thus be the his-

---

[8] In the essay, "Perpetual Peace: A Philosophical Sketch," *ibid.*, pp. 306-45, where time is not in any sense the focus of attention, a different viewpoint is implied. The great artist, nature, will produce harmony among men against their will. Man sees in this process the higher cause that predetermines the course of nature. From the point of view of our own minds we call this "providence." See pp. 322-23. "As the times required for equal steps of progress become, we hope, shorter and shorter, perpetual peace is a problem which, gradually working out its own solution, continuously approaches its goal," p. 345. Here there is moral determination by the world; perpetual peace will come even against the wills of man. Man is involved in this moral determination, he is part of it and understands it in relation to himself as "providence." One might say that moral selves are conditioned by temporal and historical existence.

tory of successive immediacies, the history of "moments" or "instants" in which the Eternal and time intersect. The self that makes a decision, like Kant's free moral self, is exempt from the determinations of history and community; it has a history as a self, but its history apparently does not in any way enter into its relation with the Eternal. It exists in Christendom, but Christendom, if it has any determination of the self, has only a negative one. "For in relation to the absolute there is only one tense: the present. . . . And as Christ is the absolute, it is easy to see that with respect to Him there is only one situation: that of contemporaneousness. . . . The eighteen hundred years are neither here nor there; they do not change Him, neither do they in any wise reveal who He was, for who He is is revealed only to faith."[10] Faith has no history; the self in faith is nonhistorical.

Like Kant's free moral self, Kierkegaard's faithful self acts in the realm of temporal determination, and its actions have consequences. As the discussion of community and time will show, the nonhistorical self in faith is obliged to obey the command to love the neighbor. The obedient actions have consequences for others, but they are motivated out of duty in faith, and not out of any real mutuality of persons.

Augustine's doctrine of the self in time casts the radical nonhistorical and individualistic character of the self in the writings of Kierkegaard and Kant into bold relief. Augustine's significance is all the greater because in understanding the historical character of the self he does not lose the relation to the eternal. The self that is timeful is also the self that in the present has a relationship with the eternal. The present in which it has a relation with the eternal is a present full of memory of the past and anticipation of the future. These memory images and expectations are not irrelevant to the soul's relation to God; they are a part of its contemporaneity. Augustine expounded this view in the context of his doctrine of creation. The radically timeful experience of human selves has been created by the Eternal who sustains that which he has created.[11]

Augustine's discussion of time in the self and the self in time is set within his doctrine of creation. In one dimension time is the order of creation, and the Creator of time is God who made all things good. Within this perspective creation is seen to be radically temporal in character. In another dimension, time is known in the human self. It is the self that recalls memory-images out of its past, and has expectations of its future. Although the self is always in the present, it knows that it has a past and a future.

---

[9] Kierkegaard, *Training in Christianity*, trans. Walter Lowrie, Princeton, 1941, p. 68. Cf. Kierkegaard, *The Concept of Dread*, trans. Lowrie, Princeton, 1944, pp. 73-83.

[10] Kierkegaard, *Training*, p. 67.

[11] Augustine, *The City of God*, Book xi, 6, *et passim*. Kant and Kierkegaard both relate the self to the absolute, but temporal and historical existence is not constitutive of the self to the extent that it is in Augustine's thought.

Out of this theory of self-knowledge of temporal existence comes Augustine's fruitful discussion of memory and of time.

In memory the self draws into the present the images of its past experiences. Not only the images of experiences are recalled, but also what is believed about the past experiences, their meanings for the self in the past. Remembered in the present, these become interpreters of the present actions of the self. Out of the past which is in the present, and the present which is present, the self projects future actions and hopes. These projections, too, are in the present.[12] Past, present, and future are all in the subject.

For if times past and to come be, I know where they be. Which yet if I cannot, yet I know, wherever they be, they are not there as future, or past, but present. For if there also they be future, they are not yet there; if there also they be past, they are no longer there. Wheresoever then is whatsoever is, it is only as present. . . . What now is clear and plain is, that neither things to come nor past are. Nor is it properly said, 'there be three times, past, present, and to come': yet perchance it might be properly said, 'there be three times; a present of things past, a present of things present, and a present of things future'. For these three do exist in some sort, in the soul, but otherwhere do I not see them; present of things past, memory; present of things present, sight; present of things future, expectation.[13]

Past, present, and future, all being in the present, mutually condition one another. Memory images interpret the present experience and hopes for the future, present sight interprets memory images and expectations; expectations interpret what memories and present experience mean for the future.

All time per se is in the present subject; thus there is no "long future," but a long expectation of the future; there is no "long past," but a long memory of the past.[14] In Augustine's understanding of the overwhelming reality of the present, there appears to be a real affinity with Kierkegaard. For both men reality is in the present. There is a crucial distinction between the present self of Kant and Kierkegaard, however, and that of Augustine. For Augustine this present has real content; it is not indeterminateness, pure freedom, or formal decision. The content of the present self is a timeful content. Its memory images and its expectations have a real quality of determinateness in the present. The self in Augustine is a profoundly historical self; it is a whole self without the sharp division between a noumenal

---

[12] Augustine, *The Confessions of St. Augustine,* trans. E. B. Pusey, New York, 1907, Book x. Cf. Book x, 14, p. 212: In memory "also meet I with myself, and recall myself, and when, where, and what I have done, and under what feelings. . . . Out of the same store do I myself with the past continually combine fresh and fresh likenesses of things, which I have experienced, or, from what I have experienced, have believed: and thence infer future actions, events, and hopes, and all these again I reflect on, as present. . . . So speak I to myself: and when I speak, the images of all I speak of are present, out of the same treasury of memory. . . ."

[13] *Ibid.,* Book xi, 23, p. 265; 26, pp. 266-67.

[14] *Ibid.,* 37, p. 274.

and a sensuous aspect. The moral self not only has temporal consequences, but the moral self is the historical self, the self that is in time, and that has time in it.[15] There can be no leap over eighteen hundred years of external history. There can be no leap out of the past and the future into a pure present. The self in the present is a self with memory images and expectations, not only immediate sight.

Because of his understanding of subjective time, how time enters into the self, Augustine contributes more significantly to an understanding of time and community than do Kant and Kierkegaard. This Augustinian notion of time becomes significant in more recent philosophy through the writings of Bergson, Royce, Dilthey, and Mead. None of these men simply mirror Augustine; in Bergson, for example, there is some affinity with Kierkegaard's notion of an immediate relation to the Ultimate. By and large, however, they are in an Augustinian stream of thought.[16]

In the writings of Henri Bergson and Josiah Royce an effort is made to develop the metaphysical consequences of a doctrine of radical temporality. Bergson's doctrine of time is unintelligible apart from his metaphysics of mobility and flux. In Royce's case, the insights into time can stand apart from his theory of the Absolute. Henri Bergson was preoccupied with Zeno's paradoxes throughout his career. In his discussion of one of the paradoxes one most succinctly gets at the heart of his metaphysics. He writes,

> In holding movement to be divisible, as its trajectory is, common sense merely expresses the two facts which alone are of importance in practical life: first, that every movement describes a space; second, that at every point of this space the moving body *might* stop. But the philosopher who reasons upon the inner nature of movement is bound to restore to it the mobility which is its essence, and this is what Zeno omits to do.[17]

Reality is finally mobility. It is known by intuition. Practical life requires that what is essentially mobile be spatialized, obstructed, and intellectualized so that we may orient our existence within it. Related sets of polarities run through his writings; the consciously structured conceptions of duration and multiplicity on the one hand, and the organic unity of living reality on the other;[18] knowledge that is thought and conscious in intelligence, and acted and unconscious in instinct;[19] metaphysics and science, intelligence and in-

[15] Cf. Augustine, *On the Trinity*, Book ix, for an indication of the way in which Augustine understood the unity of the self. Although his primary concern in this section is to show that a kind of trinity exists in man, in so doing he indicates the dynamic unity that man is.

[16] There appears to be no significant discussion of time in Augustinian terms between his writing and the nineteenth century, when there was renewed interest in "history" and "community."

[17] Bergson, *Matter and Memory*, trans. N. M. Paul and W. S. Palmer, London, 1911, p. 251.

[18] Bergson, *Time and Free Will*, trans. F. L. Pogson, London, 1910, p. 128.

[19] Bergson, *Creative Evolution*, trans. A. Mitchell, New York, 1944, pp. 160-61.

tuition, analysis and intuition;[20] closed morality and open morality, social morality and human morality, static religion and dynamic religion.[21]

In each of these polarities one has, on the one hand, an artificial construction of what is really a dynamic flow of life. The intellectualization, or the institutionalization, is necessary in order to fill the practical needs of mankind. But this process of "rationalization" is ultimately a distortion of the underlying reality that its expresses.[22] No forms can capture the dynamic of the process that creates them. On the other hand, there is a conception of an organic reality in process in which all parts flow into and through all other parts. It cannot be captured in any institutional or intellectual forms; the only way finally to know it is by intuition. It is this latter pole, the dynamic life, that is the truly real in Bergson's thought.

In Bergson's doctrine of time, the important distinction that reflects the basic polarity is that between pure duration and spatialized time. "Pure duration is the form which the succession of our conscious states assumes when our ego lets itself *live*, when it refrains from separating its present state from its former states."[23] In pure duration the past and present states are formed into an organic whole like "notes of a tune, melting, so to speak, into one another." It is "succession without distinction," "a mutual penetration, an interconnection and organization of elements, each one of which represents the whole, and cannot be distinguished or isolated from it except by abstract thought."[24] This pure duration is what Bergson calls time, "but time perceived as indivisible."[25]

The ordinary world we live in, however, is a world of spatialized time. "We have no interest in listening to the uninterrupted humming of life's depth."[26] We cannot give a practical orientation to life by listening to its hum. We must measure time against something. The inner mobility of life must be organized and systematized in some fashion in order for us to have the defined relationships with others and with nature that are necessary for an orderly society. Space is assumed in practical life to be less mobile than pure duration, and so it is against space that we measure time. Rather than understand our past as flowing into the present and interpenetrating with it, we relate our past time to other past times and places. We spatialize it,

[20] Bergson, *The Creative Mind*, trans. Mabelle L. Andison, New York, 1946, p. 49, pp. 91 ff., 190.

[21] Bergson, *The Two Sources of Morality and Religion*, trans. R. A. Audra, C. Brereton, and W. H. Carter, New York, 1935, Chs. I, II, III.

[22] Cf. Bergson, *Creative Evolution*, p. 141.

[23] Bergson, *Time and Free Will*, p. 100.

[24] *Ibid.*, p. 101.

[25] Bergson, *Creative Mind*, p. 176.

[26] *Ibid.*, "And yet, that is where real duration is. Thanks to it, the more or less lengthy changes we witness within us and in the external world, take place in a single identical time," pp. 176-77.

and objectify it in institutions and writings. Thus, our spatialized past can be manipulated; it is lifted out of the flow of which it is a part. The process of spatializing time distorts the true reality, pure duration, but the process is necessary for practical life.[27]

The line that the self draws between its past and its present is relative to the immediate interest of the self. If the immediate interest demands the re-call of the distant past, this past is present, and the line between past and present in terms of spatialized time is extended back. But as soon as our at-tention is focused on another aspect of life, the present (which may include much of the spatialized past) falls back into the past.[28]

In *Matter and Memory*, Bergson analyzes in great detail the process of memory by which the past becomes present. In this analysis we find another manifestation of the basic polarity of mobility and spatialized conceptions of mobility. *Pure memory* is part of pure duration; it is the interpenetration of the past and the present in the level of the self that exists below conscious attention. It is without practical function, and needs no explanation.[29] *Memory images* are conceptions of the past that one has in particular mo-ments of consciousness. Memory images are always in the present, and are related to the present attention of the mind. They are, in effect, spatializa-tions of pure duration. In consciousness we isolate out of the mobility which is reality (pure duration and pure memory) aspects of it that refer to our present needs and our contemplated actions.

The present is obviously not made up of memory images only; it includes perceptions. Pure perception is only theoretically possible, for every percep-tion tends to recall relevant memory images, so that immediately in con-sciousness there is an interpenetration of the two. In reverie a memory image might be recalled which in turn isolates certain aspects of the present ex-perience for perception. Thus either perception or memory images can initiate the sequence.[30]

The present self, a compound of perceptions and memory images, is always an acting self. The psychical state of the present "must be both a per-ception of the immediate past and a determination of the immediate future," it is "action or movement." Since this present is an undivided whole, the movement must be linked to the present sensation, and "prolong it in action."[31] Action unites the past, the present, and the future, for action is the focus of consciousness.

[27] Cf. *Ibid.*, p. 50.

[28] *Ibid.*, p. 179.

[29] Cf. *ibid.*, p. 180, "Memory therefore needs no explanation. Or rather, there is no special faculty whose role is to retain quantities of past in order to pour it into the present. The past preserves itself automatically."

[30] Bergson, *Matter and Memory*, pp. 74-75.

[31] *Ibid.*, p. 177.

Consciousness then, illumines, at each moment of time, that immediate part of the past which, impending over the future, seeks to realize and to associate with it. Solely preoccupied in thus determining an undetermined future, consciousness may shed a little of its light on those of our states, more remote in the past, which can be usefully combined with our present state, that is to say, with our immediate past: the rest remains in the dark. It is in this illuminated part of our history that we remain seated, in virtue of the fundamental law of life, which is the law of action. . . .[32]

There are significant affinities between Bergson's understanding of the self and time, and that of Augustine. For both, the present is the reality; it is determined by the focus of attention, the consciousness of the self. The past and the future become part of the present, the past in memory images, and the future in contemplated actions. Memory images, contemplation of the future, and present sensations interpret one another, all in the living present. But there are significant differences between the thought of Bergson and Augustine. The present existence of the self is not static but dynamic in Augustine's theory; and it is sustained by its eternal (timeless) Creator. For Bergson the present consciousness is really a spatialization and distortion of the ultimate reality of mobility that underlies it. The ultimate reality can be known intuitively, and insofar as a self can be divorced from practical concerns, symbols, and concepts, it can have knowledge of this mobility. Thus the self acting as metaphysician (in Bergson's sense of the term) is somewhat similar to the time-transcending free self that one finds in the works of Kant and Kierkegaard. The self for Bergson does not have to relate itself to reality through spatialized time; it can have an immediate relation with the truly real.[33] In intuition the self is not determined by the present, nor by the past and future in the present. It becomes a really free self as it extracts itself from an awareness of its spatialized temporality, and intuits its pure duration.[34] Thus for this aspect of the existence of the self, there can be no significant community. Intuition is individualistic.

Josiah Royce's theory about the way in which temporal existence with its memories and expectations is constitutive of community is developed analogously from his view of the temporal character of selfhood. Royce's doctrines of the self, community, and time can be separated from his idealistic metaphysics without distorting their significance.[35] Since the metaphysical position is tangential to the present concern, a discussion of it is omitted.

Royce all through his career was concerned about the two problems of time and community. One finds in some of his early essays, published in *Fugitive Essays*,[36] clear indications of trends that culminated in *The Prob-*

---

[32] *Ibid.*, p. 194.

[33] Cf. Bergson, *The Creative Mind*, pp. 150-51, 190-91, 36-37.

[34] Bergson speaks of the "joy of philosophy," *ibid.*, p. 152.

[35] See John E. Smith, *Royce's Social Infinite*, pp. 13 ff., for a summary of the development of the theory of the Absolute in Royce's thought.

[36] Royce, *Fugitive Essays*, intro. J. Loewenberg, Cambridge, 1920. Cf. p. 253,

lem of Christianity. The analysis of time and the self is, however, made in the latter book. As was pointed out in the text of the present book, Royce understood community to be essentially the result of the time process. So also, "a self is, by its very essence, a being with a past."[37] The self is and has a history; what one understands himself to be now is inseparably bound to his understanding of his former life. At any given moment only a mere fragment of the total self is present, for the self is both its past and its future. "In brief, my ideal of myself is an interpretation of my past,— linked also with an interpretation of my hopes and intentions as to my future."[38] Not only is the self a history to itself, but a person "in great part is, for his fellowmen, a record."[39] Not only does the self define itself according to its past, but others interpret the present self by virtue of its past actions, values, and qualifications. Past and future are part of the self through the process of interpretation.

Wilhelm Dilthey, like Bergson, was impressed by the dynamic character of life. For him temporality is a basic category for understanding humanity and its history.[40] Unlike Bergson, however, Dilthey is not interested in working out a metaphysics of time. He is a philosopher of human life and history. His concern is with the *Geisteswissenschaften*, the human or cultural studies. The temporal character of human life and human history, not the dynamic mobility of ultimate reality, is a focus of Dilthey's attention.

Dilthey's doctrine of time and the self is like Augustine's. Time is the basis of the possiblity of a unity in human consciousness. In the present the restless movement of time draws both the past and the future into the particular moment. The present is the filling of a moment of time with reality.[41] Only the present is really existent; it is lived, whereas the past is present only in memory and the future in anticipation, in wishes, hopes, expectations, and fears. The living, filled present continues constantly, but the content of the present continually changes.[42]

Dilthey's analysis of why and how the self in the present orders its past and its future, is significant. The self can look both backward and forward. Looking backward, the memory images come to consciousness according to

---

"Now we advance the view that past and future and the timeflow are all of them notions expressing something meant by a present thought-activity. They are projections, so to speak, of the present content of consciousness, by an act of thought whose nature must be judged from an immediate perception of its working."

[37] Royce, *The Problem of Christianity*, II, p. 40.

[38] *Ibid.*, p. 42.

[39] *Ibid.*, p. 43.

[40] Dilthey, *Gesammelte Schriften*, Vol. VII, p. 192. My discussion of self and time in Dilthey's thought comes largely from this volume, pp. 191-204.

[41] Cf. John Marsh, *The Fulness of Time*, London, 1952, *passim*, for a discussion of "filled time" as a Biblical concept.

[42] Dilthey, *op. cit.*, pp. 192-93.

the meaning that they have for us. The category of meaning (*Bedeutung*) is crucial in the whole enterprise of the human studies.[43]

Meaning determines what the self remembers, and how it interprets the memory images. This meaning is always rooted in the existing present. Insofar as the actions of the past are irrevocable, man is passive in relation to the past. In relation to the future, however, he is active and free. The present, opening toward the future, is filled with actuality and with possibility; man acts in relation to this possibility. The category for understanding our relation to the future, then, is purpose, for purpose is realized in the life of the future that possibly can emerge out of the present actuality.[44]

The present is never experienced without the past and the future. The present has a certain duration that distinguishes it from the past and the future; this duration is determined by the consciousness of a unity, or a character of inseparability that includes all that is present in the consciousness. The unity of the present has a structure, and the structure and extent of the duration are related to the value, negative and positive, that the self imposes upon that which it draws into unity.[45] Thus the category of value (*Wert*) is the category of the present. But what one grasps in the present consciousness is not life itself; it is a configuration (*Gestaltung*) of life which has a meaningful unity in relation to the grasping self. When consciousness is fixed on the flux of life that flows through the present, one objectifies from this flux and holds fast particular aspects of it.[46] Dilthey significantly differs from Bergson at this point; the objectified configurations of inner experience are not distortions of life. They are not lived experience itself, but they become the means by which one can return to the inner character of lived experience of the past.

The categories of meaning, value, and purpose, which refer to the past, the present, and the future, have no given order in relation to one another. All three are useful in understanding and interpreting experience. They are related to three aspects of the self: memory, feeling, and volition. In giving unity to the experiences of one's life, however, the category of meaning (*Bedeutung*), which has reference to memory, becomes the most important. The center of meaning determines the interpretation of the past and its continuity with the present in the life-process. The unity of the dynamic present exists because it has meaning with reference to some value. Dilthey illustrates the centrality of the category of meaning in drawing memory images and anticipations into the present by referring to three autobiographies. The point of meaning that gives coherence and unity to Augustine's life, and thus to his autobiography (the literary expression of self-conscious-

[43] *Ibid.*, pp. 232-41, 198-99.
[44] *Ibid.*, pp. 201-2.
[45] *Ibid.*, pp. 230-3ʹ, 194.
[46] *Ibid.*, pp. 241-43, 201-2.

ness of meaning in one's life), is the understanding of his own being in relation to God. All of his life had meaning around this central relationship, which he knew out of a past event, his conversion. The unity of Rousseau's life lies in the value of being a sympathetic humanitarian, an ideal common to his time. Goethe's central meaning was the development and configuration, or evolution of life. The autobiographies of these men illustrate the way in which the present has a unity of past and future, or memory and expectation, in relation to a meaning, a value, or a purpose.[47] Meaning, however, is the most illuminating. Through the integrating center of meaning (*Bedeutungszusammenhang*), parts of lived experience are related to the whole. Through it the unity of consciousness, which is the unity of the self, exists. The center of meaning interprets in a pattern the past, the present, and the future for the self.[48]

In Dilthey's theory, as in the thought of Bergson and Royce, the past and future enter into the present existence of the self. The values of the present, the meaning of memories of the past, and the purposes of the future are bound together in an integrating center of meaning. In an analogous fashion the memory and expectation of a community become part of its present.

Like Dilthey, George Herbert Mead is not concerned with the metaphysical consequences of his theory of time. For Mead the purpose of thought was to interpret and anticipate experience. Mead dealt with the three problems of time, self, and community, and he analyzed each with great insight. However, he asked somewhat different questions of human experience from what we are asking, for he has no explicit discussion of the three in interrelationship. In his social theory of the self he does not explicitly consider the dimension of time. In his detailed discussion of time, he does not bring to bear his social theory of the self in any formal way.[49]

In Mead's theory of time there is a strong definition of the exclusive reality of the present, and the unreality of the past. "The present of course implies a past and a future, and to these both we deny existence."[50] This sweeping statement makes a consistent interpretation of Mead difficult, for although he denies that memory refers to "events having a reality inde-

[47] *Ibid.*, pp. 198, 196-202.
[48] Dilthey distinguishes between lived time, with its fullness of dynamic content in the self, and mathematical time of the natural sciences. The latter, like the concepts of causality and space, is foreign to the human studies apart from considerable redefinition. Cf. *ibid.*, pp. 192-93.
[49] Cf. Mead, *The Philosophy of the Present*, especially pp. 1-31; "The Nature of the Past," in *Essays in Honor of John Dewey*, New York, 1929, pp. 235-42. There are scattered discussions of the theory of time in *The Philosophy of the Act*, Chicago, 1938. The essay, "Passage, Process, and Permanance," pp. 321-56, is the most important treatment of time in that book. Cf. also Maurice Nathanson, "George H. Mead's Metaphysic of Time," *Journal of Philosophy*, Vol. 50 (1953), pp. 770-82.
[50] *The Philosophy of the Present*, p. 1.

pendent of the present,"[51] nevertheless the self does have memories of the past. The past refers "to such an interpretation of the present in its conditioning passage as will enable intelligent conduct to proceed." The materials out of which the past is constructed lie in the present, making it impossible to appeal to a real past "to which we may recur to check up our constructions."[52] While affirming this radically present character of the past, he states that these reconstructions of the past can change in different presents. This cannot be said, however, without inferring that the reconstructions *of the past* refer to something that exists in at least partial independence from the present. It is *the past* that is reconstructed. Yet this inference Mead chooses to deny. In the end, however, he is forced to admit the existence of the past; the past is "mental," just as the future is mental. Consciousness of the past, just as imagination of the future, is always a mental present. "The novelty of every future demands a novel past."[53] In the duration of the present we are attempting to reconstruct a past that enables us to control the present and interpret the future. Yet all three, past, present, and future, are in the present.

From this theory of time, it would appear that the self existing in the present is a radically free self; it is free to reconstruct its own past almost as it wishes. In Mead's theory of the "I" and "me" aspects of the self, however, the determinations posited in the "me" are of great significance.[54] In the theory of the self in *Mind, Self, and Society*, the self is to a large extent conditioned by its own past, and the expectations of others (the role of the generalized other).[55] Although the "I" aspect of the self acts, responds, and is free, the past actions and responses form a structure of attitude which limits and conditions the "I." This structure is the "me."[56] Unlike the unreality of the past in the theory of time, in the theory of the self the past is carried into every present in such a way as largely to determine the possible actions and responses. The past does exist in the "me." It is also carried by the significant symbols and their meanings through which the self comes to being in a community.

All of these philosophers in the "Augustinian stream" indicate properly that being in time is an important aspect of being a self. Past experiences, or personal history, enter into what a person is in a given moment. They are part of the persisting aspects of the self that emerge out of changing experiences. At times memory images come to consciousness by the provocation of the present experiences of the self. They enter into the interpretation of

[51] *Ibid.*, p. 29.
[52] *Ibid.*
[53] *Ibid.*, p. 31.
[54] *Mind, Self, and Society*, pp. 173 ff.
[55] Cf., *The Philosophy of the Present*, pp. 176 ff.
[56] *Mind, Self, and Society*, p. 174. "As given, it is a 'me,' but it is a 'me' which was the 'I' at the earlier time."

this experience so that the past lives within the present. On other occasions memory images evoke present experience by drawing attention to aspects of the milieu of physical and social reality in which persons exist. As with the past, so with the future. Expectations are developed out of memories of the past and the possibilities of the present. In turn they help to interpret the present and the past by their existence in the self. This is the wisdom of Augustine and those who have in some sense shared and developed the idea that time exists in and for selves.

Community and Time

In what sense does the subjective meaning of experience in time enter into the inner life of a community? The question may be asked in a different way. Given the reality of an inner unity of meaning in community, is this meaning related only to immediate experience, or is temporality (or history) an essential part of a community? In one sense the answer is obvious. The difference between a crowd and a community is in part that a crowd finds unity in an immediate experience that is the center of attention for many individuals, whereas the members of a community have a unity that may persist through generations and does not have an explicit immediate focus. How the temporal character of a community becomes essential to its existence, however, is a problem that has not been widely explored. If unsophisticated group mind theories are rejected, i.e., theories which posit an independent existence to a social mental unity, an alternative understanding needs to be developed. One possible approach is through analogies to theories of time and the self. The way in which men understand the self in time appears to have consequences for their understanding of community.

There are similarities between Kant and Kierkegaard on the problem of how a self relates itself to another as well as in their theories of the essentially nontimeful self. For both there is a law to which free selves are bound in obedience, and through which they relate themselves to the other. In Kant's theory of the moral life, there is a natural moral law, a formal ethical principle that is objective to the moral actors. Of itself it is not the incentive to moral action. It does not give maxims which are internalized for the guidance of the actor in a particular situation. It is not "the subjective determining ground" of the will. Only in respect or reverence for the moral law does morality itself take form.[57] Once internalized, the moral law is the formal

[57] *Critique of Practical Reason*, pp. 176-95. See pp. 183-84, "Since the ideal of the moral law deprives self-love of its influence and self-conceit of its delusion, it lessens the obstacle to pure practical reason and produces the idea of the superiority of its objective law to the impulses of sensibility. . . . Thus respect for the law is not the incentive to morality; it is morality itself, regarded subjectively as an incentive, inasmuch as pure practical reason, by rejecting all the rival claims of self-love, gives authority and absolute sovereignty to the law." Paton uses "reverence" rather than "respect."

principle through which the self is related to the other. Duty requires that actions conform to the moral law. In the moral life persons are related to one another through obedience to the moral law which, in part, demands that they respect one another.

This theory of moral community is the logical outcome of the theory of the moral self. Kant does not deny that selves are related to one another in the realm of consequences of decisions. The world of sense is the world of cause and effect, and in this world the actions of one impinge upon another through the laws of natural order, as we understand them. But the essence of the self is autonomous; at the deepest level the self is free, and enters into relationships with the other through its sense of obligation not to the person, but to the moral law. "Respect for the moral law is therefore the sole and undoubted moral incentive. . . ."[58] The doctrine of the transcendent free self means that in the end there is no real mutuality of selves; individual autonomous selves are related to one another only through their common sense of obligation to a formal moral principle.

The dimension of a common past cannot bring persons together in community, for time is of the order of the sensuous, and the true self transcends time. There is no significant determination of the self by its own past, its memories, in the moral life. If this is the case it is impossible for selves to be related to one another through memories that are common to them. Doctrines of self and time and community are integrally related, at least by implication.

Kierkegaard's understanding of the self in decision about the moment in which eternity and time intersect leads to a conception of community much like that implicit in Kant's theory. The law through which selves are related to one another, however, is not so formal in character as in Kant's moral law. It is historical in the sense that it was given in history with the particular historical moment that Kierkegaard absolutizes, the event Jesus Christ. Kierkegaard wrote, "If it were not a duty to love, then the concept of the neighbor would not exist. . . ."[59] The law through which the self who has decided to be contemporaneous with Christ is related to the neighbor is the law of love. "In loving your neighbor you are united with God,"[60] but you are really not united with your neighbor. This, to Kierkegaard, is the glory of his conception of love, for the neighbor you love is such an abstraction that none of his conditions as an historical person makes any difference. Your temporally undetermined self is related in "love" (really in obedience to

[58] *Ibid.*, p. 186. The moral law, however, demands respect for persons. "Act so that you treat humanity, whether in your own person or in that of another, always as an end and never as a means only." "Foundation of the Metaphysics of Morals," *ibid.*, p. 87.

[59] Kierkegaard, *Works of Love*, trans. D. F. and L. M. Swenson, Princeton, 1946, p. 37.

[60] *Ibid.*, p. 54.

a law of love) to the temporally undetermined self of the other through the decision to be obedient to the commandment to love the neighbor. Neither your personal history nor his enters into the relationship. Neither the community of which you are a part nor his enters into the relationship. The curious effect of this is that the great philosopher of existence is involved in such separation of "existence" from actual life that community becomes a lifeless abstraction of timeless selves united by a formal principle.

Ironically, probably neither Kant nor Kierkegaard would have had the interest to develop their theories of the moral life apart from being members of timeful communities. The pietistic legalism in Kant's social background has often been stressed. For his very efforts to call Christendom to Christianity, Kierkegaard was dependent upon the provocation of Bishop Mynster and the historical situation of the Danish Church. The self of neither of these men was as autonomous as they believed the self of everyman to be. Contrary to Kant and Kierkegaard, the self is in time, and in community; it is in a community which is in time. Those who have affinities with the Augustinian theory of the self in time tend to develop a theory of community that throws the individualism of Kant and Kierkegaard into bold relief.

In the discussion of Bergson's theory of the self and time, an important affinity with Kant and Kierkegaard was noted. In Bergson's theory the intuiting self that immediately apprehends pure duration is essentially a timeless self. Yet for other purposes of the self, time is taken seriously; the self is involved in history. There are two possible conceptions of community within Bergson's thought, depending on whether one begins with the self as metaphysician or as practical, with the timeless self or the temporal self. We have noted that in his earlier writings he held that the intellectual, structured, institutionalized manifestations of life are antithetical to the immediate, intuited understanding of pure reality. In later writings he indicated that the structured forms of life are necessary for the continuation of dynamic new impulses of life.

In the dynamic flow of life—pure duration—all life interpenetrates all other life, all time interpenetrates all other time, and all selves interpenetrate all other selves. Thus, one can say that in Bergson's thought there is a unity of selves already in existence. This unity of life, however, leaves no place for community, that is, the relation of selves who are "terminal individuals." Bergson's theory does not allow for any ultimate individuality of aspects of life. To reduce life to a unity of dynamic energy is ultimately to deny the existence of discrete individuals as we know them in experience in history and in social life. Perhaps the source of Bergson's analogy at this point causes this difficulty. An interpretation of life from a basically biological perspective is bound to come to a different position on unity and individuality from one that has the moral experience of human history as its guide.

The way in which historical selves could have community within Bergson's unity of life is in some respects similar to the meaning of community in Kant and Kierkegaard. For the intuiting self there is no significant relationship to the other person, per se, but many individuals can relate themselves intuitively to the common stream of life of which each is a part. Only the structure of the relationship is similar to Kant and Kierkegaard; selves are not really related to one another, but are all related to a common center. The center in Bergson's case is not an objective moral law to which selves are obedient, but the flow of life which is common in the end to all of life. Kant, Kierkegaard, and Bergson all end in individualism. Intuition is an individualistic way of knowing. Intuition is the basis upon which knowledge of the common reality of life is known in Bergson's theoretical framework.

In Bergson's remarks about practical life, however, there is recognition that relations between selves must be organized and structured.[61] Spatialized time is as necessary for the maintenance of human life as is pure duration. The past is deposited in customs, institutions, and language, all of which are necessary for a commodity to exist in history. Social life needs spatialized time in order to function; it needs collective representations in order to keep alive the inner spirit of a community. The self has practical needs, as well as a relation to the pure duration and the vitality that undergirds it. The ordering of community, however, is a distortion of the real life. For Bergson the truly real is the dynamic and unformed interpenetration of each in each and all in all. Nevertheless, the self with its memory images that draw its past into the interpretation of the active present is as much a part of life as the self that intuitively and immediately knows pure duration. The self is related to other selves through customs and institutions that have come into being through the years. There is unity not only in the interpenetration of the final unity, the life stream of which all are part, but also in historical life in which we relate ourselves to one another through special forms.

Bergson discussed the self and the unity of selves at these two levels. They involve two theories or at least aspects of the self. They involve two theories or aspects of time, and issue in two forms of unity or community. His theory of the function of myths, customs, and institutions sheds light on the way in which the past events and their meanings for particular historical communities can become constituent parts of the contemporary unity of a group. These things are expressions of spiritual impulses in the society. In a sense they are the spatializations of pure duration which includes all of time. Through them the community maintains the meaning of its past in the present generation.

In the thought of Josiah Royce, community is the product of a time

[61] Cf. Bergson, *Two Sources*, p. 257, "But just as the new moral aspiration takes shape only by borrowing from the closed society its natural form, which is obligation, so dynamic religion is propagated only through images and symbols supplied by the myth-making function."

process. Insofar as its members share an event as their common past, as an event in the personal history of each, it is a community of memory. Insofar as they share personally in the anticipation of an event, it is a community of expectation or hope.[62] The language is Augustinian; memory images and expectations are in the present. The inner life that gives unity to a social group, that makes it a community, then, is always in the present. To show the significance of the present in a community, two other aspects of Royce's theory must be noted. The community acts; it is not simply the accretion of a time process. The past that is shared is a past that has relevance for current action. "Common objects belong to a community only when these objects are bound up with the deeds of the community."[63] That which draws the past and the future into focus in the present is common action. If it is possible for a community to act in the present, it can achieve consensus and make decisions from among possible alternatives. Community, which is essentially a time process, must have some self-consciousness in order to act. On the one hand, the demand for a present deed draws the community into a new level of self-consciousness of its existence, informed by memory and anticipation. On the other hand, community could not act in the present apart from a self-consciousness that exists in part because of common memory and common hope. In short, the relationship between self-consciousness and corporate action is dialectical.

Corporate action, however, does not of itself bring community into existence. Much corporate action is at the level of utility only; this does not create the inner unity of meaning that is at the heart of true community. Utilitarian action may over a long time-span lead to community, for out of continuous corporate action a common past and a sense of common destiny grow. The dimension in the present that transforms utilitarian action into community is love, or loyalty. This love depends "upon seeking in the successful cooperation of all the members precisely that event which the individual member most eagerly loves as his own fulfillment.[64]

In the present the community is not only acting and loving, but also interpreting. Just as the present self interprets the past self to the future self, so the community in the present interprets its past to its future. The process again is dialectical. In the light of present action it interprets past and future; in the light of its past it interprets present and future; in the light of its hope it interprets past and present.[65] Through the process of interpretation, the past and future of a community become part of its common subjective existence in the present.[66]

[62] Royce, *The Problem of Christianity*, II, pp. 3-53.
[63] *Ibid.*, p. 65.
[64] *Ibid.*, p. 92; cf. also Royce, *The Philosophy of Loyalty*, New York, 1908, pp. 107 ff., especially, pp. 118-19.
[65] Royce, *Problem*, II, pp. 144-46.
[66] Royce, in his threefold emphasis on the timeful character of community, the

Royce's understanding of the way in which the process of interpretation of signs brings the past and the future into the present sheds light not only on how time enters into community, but also how community persists through time. Signs that are objective to the subjective life of the community are expressions of the meanings of past events and expectations of the future. Through their interpretation, past and future become present; through them the possibility of common meaning persisting through time exists. Meanings of past events are delineated in signs. The signs serve the same function that myth, customs, language, and institutions serve in Bergson's conception of the myth-making function of society. Significant symbols in G. H. Mead's theory of society, and expressions or objectifications of lived experience in Wilhelm Dilthey's theory of history, have similar functions. They are expressions of meanings common to a community. Through the processes of communication, interpretation, and understanding, the meanings of the signs can be reappropriated in each generation.

A past event can be common within a community because the event and its meaning have been defined in a sign. This goes on in all the religions, and according to Royce can be seen particularly at work in the Christian community. There is continuity between the Pauline Church and the Old Testament community through the interpretation of the history of the people of Israel that became part of the meaning of the life of the new community.[67] In a time when much of Protestantism was concerned to restore the "religion of Jesus," Royce wrote,

> Historically speaking, Christianity has never appeared simply as the religion taught by the Master. It has always been an interpretation of the master and of his religion in the light of some doctrine concerning God, man, and man's salvation. . . .[68]

The event of Jesus Christ was interpreted in signs, which were further interpreted in the community as it lived on through history. The principal

---

community of deed and of interpretation, has as his ultimate focus of attention the Absolute. In the Absolute the past, present, and future are one with action and interpretation. For our purposes we find Royce's understanding of community and time to be significant for interpreting the Christian community apart from the metaphysics involved.

[67] Royce, *Problem*, II, p. 38.

[68] *Ibid.*, I, p. 25. Cf. "But the parables, the symbols, the historical incidents that the religious imagination uses in its portrayals,—these are the more or less sacred and transient *accidents* in which the 'real presence' of the divine at once shows itself to us, and hides the detail of its inner life from us. These accidents of the religious imagination endure through many ages; but they also vary. . . . Whoever sees the living truth of the personal and conscious and ethical unity of the world *through* these symbols is possessed of the absolute religion, whatever his nominal creed or church. Whoever overemphasizes the empirical details of these symbols, and then asks us to accept these details as literally true, commits an error. . . ." Royce, *The Philosophy of Loyalty*, p. 397.

signs of the event, however, are limitations of the meaning of the event for the early community. These are the New Testament and the Apostles' Creed. Objectively given to each generation in the Church, these signs bear the possibility of inner continuity of meaning through history. They evoke interpretations of human experience in the light of the given meaning of the past event. Through the interpretation of signs, the past event becomes part of the present life of the community. Through the continued existence of the signs of the event, there is continuity of interpretation through history which makes possible a unity of meaning through time.

Wilhelm Dilthey held that the basic spirit of a period or a people is expressed in objective mind, that is, in their arts, philosophy, value systems, economic organizations, and religious life. Through the processes of sympathetic subjective understanding these objectifications of lived experience can be the mediators for reliving and reconstructing the inner life of the past.

Dilthey rejects the two extremes of atomistic individuality and community mind (*Volksgeist*) as adequate conceptions of the relation of the individual mind to the group. He noted that the analogy of organism is most frequently put forward to explain the latter, but rejects this analogy because we do not know any more about organisms than we do about society. Also, one of the key marks of "mind" is the existence of an apperceptive unity which cannot be found in a social body.[69] Yet groups have unity. Dilthey believed, much as Royce did, that common memories, common ends, and common experiences are a reality in groups. The individual makes the goals of a group his own, he experiences the nation's experiences as his own, and the memory of these is preserved in his personal memory.[70]

The unity of a period or a group is characterized by prevailing great tendencies that go through the life of the times and the community. The minds of men are filled with common ideas and values which to some extent they all pursue. A common spirit is manifest in all the activity of individuals and the group;[71] in such a variety of expressions as the prevailing style of life, the economic order, the systems of purposes and values that the society has formed for itself, morality, law, the state, religion, art, science and philosophy. These expressions of life are the objectified forms of the common spiritual and cultural background. They are the *Objektive Geist*, the objective mind of the group. These objectifications come into existence through individuals and groups of persons who are active in the period. Even the work of greatest individuality, that of genius, expresses the common spirit. The objective mind forms the factors that are common to both I and Thou, and thus makes unity of meaning possible. It impinges upon the child

[69] Dilthey, *Gesammelte Schriften*, Vol. I, Leipzig and Berlin, 1923, pp. 29 ff. Cf. Vol. V, Leipzig and Berlin, 1924, pp. 62-63.
[70] *Ibid.*, Vol. VII, pp. 282 ff.
[71] *Ibid.*, p. 177 ff.

before he learns to speak, and continues to exist in the world within which the mature individual orients himself.[72]

Objective mind expresses the dynamic process of history and life itself. The unity of meaning, ultimately a nonrational unity, takes concrete form in the varieties of cultural life.[73] The structure of objective mind is in some sense an expression of the structure of the inner unity of the period or community out of which it emerged. For Dilthey, the concretions of spirit are not necessarily distorted forms of the underlying reality. They express the underlying reality with real sensitivity and validity. Because there is an inner relation between the objectification and the living reality expressed by it, objective mind becomes the medium by which we are able to relive (*nacherleben*), understand (*verstehen*), and reconstruct (*nachbilden*) the inner life of the past.[74] It is through objective mind that we are able to make the lived experience (*Erlebnis*) of the past a part of our own lived experience.

Though the common meaning of a community is related to its past through the understanding of the past as it is expressed in the objectifications of lived experience, the present is the focus of common meaning. The present meaning both conditions and is conditioned by common memories. On the one hand, an event in the present life of the community will tend to evoke and select certain aspects of the life of the past that are relevant to contemporary experience. On the other hand, the memory of past events becomes part of the interpretation of present experience. In reference to the possibility of fulfilling purposes in the present, both meaning and value are present. What is important in the present (value) conditions the selection of purposes and goals for the community in the open future. In turn both are interpreted and understood in light of the meaning of the past history of the community. Further, the purposes of the future enter into the interpretation of both the values of the present and the meaning of the past. The meanings, values, and purposes, however, that are in the consciousness of the community at a given time never fully encompass the totality of dynamic lived experience. They are selected out of the totality of experience. Yet apart from the objectification of particular centers of meaning out of lived experience, the totality of life would be incoherent and unorganized. Par-

[72] *Ibid.*, pp. 208-209, pp. 156-57.

[73] Cf. Karl Mannheim, *Essays on the Sociology of Knowledge*, ed. P. Kecskemeti, London, 1952, pp. 37-42, for an interpretation of Dilthey's theory of *Weltanschauung*. Much of Mannheim's early work, translated in this and other volumes, is germane to this discussion. There are two useful general introductions to Dilthey's philosophy in English: H. A. Hodges, *Wilhelm Dilthey, An Introduction*, New York, 1944, and Hodges, *The Philosophy of Wilhelm Dilthey*, London, 1952. A remarkable concise introduction is O. F. Bollnow, *Dilthey, Eine Einführung in seine Philosophie*, Stuttgart, 1955.

[74] Dilthey, Vol. VII, pp. 210-20, also *"Die Kategorien des Lebens,"* pp. 228-45.

ticular centers of meaning become the focus for the interpretation of life, past, present, and future, in a community.

The center of meaning that organizes lived experience (*Bedeutungszusammenhang*) enters into the expression of that experience in every form. History is written in a fashion analogous to autobiography; there is a present meaning that conditions the way in which the history of both the present and the past is written. Such a meaning enters into the definition of the expectations of a community. Art, philosophy, and religious life also express certain meanings, values, and purposes that are current in a community. Thus the expressions of the past lived experience of a community have a configuration (*Gestaltung*) centering in a common and more or less dominant meaning. Through the expressions of the meaning of the experience of the past, men in the present can again enter into this meaning of the past. Because humanity has common dimensions of experience throughout history, and because this experience is expressed in, and interpreted by, various of its objectifications, the past can become part of the present through the process of understanding. Because the expressions of past lived experience are objective to their particular interpretations and meanings for any given time, they tend to preserve to a large extent the possibility of a common interpretation. Continuity of inner meaning within community is possible because certain expressions of the past experience of the community are cherished and sympathetically understood through time. Certain of these signs can carry the center of meaning for the organization and interpretation of the life of a community in any time, and thus determine the characteristic meanings of the community through history.

We have seen how the function of signs in the philosophy of Royce, objectifications in Dilthey, and the myth-making function in Bergson are in general similar. They make possible both the presence of the past in the contemporary life of a community, and the continuity of meaning through time. Although G. H. Mead made an effort to deny the reality of the past, in his theory of communication significant symbols and the "me" aspect of the self make real the presence of the past. Symbols are significant only when they bear meaning in the present for both parties involved in communication. While in one dimension the meaning is in the present moment of experience, in another dimension the symbol carries meaning from the past through the present and into the future of the community. Symbols can evoke common meanings from both parties because the parties share a common experience and common history out of which the symbol has emerged. Language, for example, has significance in the present because it bears meanings out of the past life of the community that uses it.[75] Language is

---

[75] Mead, *Mind, Self, and Society*, pp. 261-62, 268, 173, *et passim*. E.g., "A person is a personality because he belongs to a community, because he takes over the institutions of that community into his own conduct. He takes its language as

not novel, it has developed through the history of the community; out of this history comes the possibility of its significance for the present. In a similar fashion, institutions are the encrustations of actions in the past of a community. They carry past patterns of action into contemporary experience, and in this way make the past meanings of experience present. The experiential dimension of meaning is in the present, but its presence is dependent upon symbols and institutions that are objective to present experience. Through the process of communication the meanings of these symbols become contemporary. They would have no meaning apart from the present communication, yet communication in the present depends upon symbols that carry meaning from the past into the present. Within Mead's discussion, symbols do not carry the meanings of crucial events and the basic global outlook of a people as much as they do in the theories of Royce and Dilthey. Rather, they stimulate common responses. Even at this level, however, the past becomes present through the internalization of meanings of symbols that exist objective to the contemporary generation and experience.

For Mead, the past is present not only in significant symbols and institutions, but also in the self that emerges out of social experience and communication. Communication rests not only on common symbols, but also upon the fact that many persons share in the meaning of these symbols. As the self emerges in social experience, knowing and guiding itself with reference to the generalized other, the society of which it is a part, it takes on the meanings of its society. Certain patterns of meaning which arise out of past experiences and actions become part of the abiding self, the "me." The experiences that develop the "me" are not atomistically individual; they are social in character. Through them the past responses common to the community become the present responses of individual selves. Even the free actions of the "I" aspect of the self are to some extent conditioned by the internalization of the past of the community in the present of the self. They are expressed and interpreted in the symbols of the community. Through the existence of the common symbols, the meanings that are common to many persons are the meanings coming out of the past of the community.

From the reflections of these men the basic thesis of Chapters 4, 5, 6, and part of 7, of the present book was developed. The unity of a community at any given time and through history is at least bi-polar. On the one hand, it centers in persons who share common meanings and interpretations of experience that come out of the past. On the other hand, it centers in the objective external expressions of these meanings from the past given in art,

---

a medium by which he gets his personality, and then through the process of taking the different roles that all the others furnish he comes to get the attitude of the members of the community. Such, in a certain sense, is the structure of a man's personality," p. 162. Cf. "The Genesis of the Self and Social Control," in *The Philosophy of the Present*, pp. 176-95.

documents, and other signs and expressions of lived experience. These objectifications are not entirely dependent for their existence upon the existence of particular persons in a community. However, they would have no meaning and significance apart from the internalization of their meaning in persons who make up the community. The internalization processes are the processes of interaction and mental activity we have interpreted under communication, interpretation, understanding commitment, and action.[76] These objectifications carry the past into the present, and carry the unity of the community through time.

[76] Cf. H. R. Niebuhr, *The Meaning of Revelation*, New York, 1941, especially pp. 43-90. "External history is the medium in which internal history exists and comes to life," p. 90. A distinct merit of this bi-polar view is that it avoids the hypostatization of a "group mind," and yet accounts for the same phenomena that such a notion does.

Index

Action: function of, in the Church, 12, 91-97; forms of, in the Church, 12, 93 ff.

Adams, James Luther, 29

Allen, Joseph L., 31

Anonymity, and the function of the Church, 25

Augustine, 73, 114, 117-119, 122

Baptism: as "initiation rite," 16-17; as celebration of birth, 17

Barth, Karl, 110, 111, 112

Belief, 89-93

Bergson, Henri, 114, 119-122, 123, 125, 129, 130

Bible: as source of Church's language, 46-50; diversity of "languages" in, 46-49; selectivity of use, 48-50; as object of interpretation, 58-59; its function in "common memory," 74-78

Bonhoeffer, D., 13, 112

Brunner, Emil, 29, 103

Cayton, Horace, 25

Church: defined as a human community, 3, 6; meeting natural needs, 7-8, 14 ff.; meeting physical needs, 15, 16-19; meeting psychological needs, 15, 19-21; meeting social needs, 15, 21-28; as political institution, 8-9, 28-42; as language community, 9-10, 45-55; as community of interpretation, 10-11, 56-71; as community of understanding (*Verstehen*) and memory, 11, 72-81; as community of loyalty, 11-12; as community of action, 12, 91-97; differentiated from other communities, 13; seen from religious viewpoint, 104-105; theological compared to social approach to,

105-106; theological approach to social interpretation of, 108-112

Church History, social function of, 80-81

Church Year, as recovery of memory, 73-74

Clark, W. H., 19

Communication, 45-55; function of, in sustaining community, 50-52

Communion, social function of, 78-80

Community: working definition of, 1; and time, 127-137; in Kierkegaard's thought, 128-129; in Bergson's thought, 129-130; in Royce's thought, 130-133; in Dilthey's thought, 133-135; in G. H. Mead's thought, 135-136

Confirmation, as "initiation rite," 16-17

Continuity of Church, 42-45; as a function of language, 51-52; as a function of memory and understanding, 81-85

Cotton, J. H., 73

Covenant, as a social act, 86-87

Creeds, social function of, 52-53

Cushman, Robert E., 113

Death, as occasion for religious life, 18

Dillistone, F. W., 86

Dilthey, Wilhelm, 11, 74, 114, 119, 123-125, 132, 133-135, 136

Drake, St. Claire, 25

Durkheim, Emile, 16, 22, 44

Eating, as occasion of religious significance, 18

Ecumenical Movement, political forms of, 36-38

Evangelism: social function of, 67-69; as common action, 95-96; as divisive, 98